To Two Fanatical fans

Journey

from **to** the VERY GREAT

Justice

State of Washington!

A Story of Fierce Independence
in Politics and in Life

Carol & Glenn; I am glad you are my friends!

NORMAN
GOLDMAN

Norm

P.S. I hope you like the book!

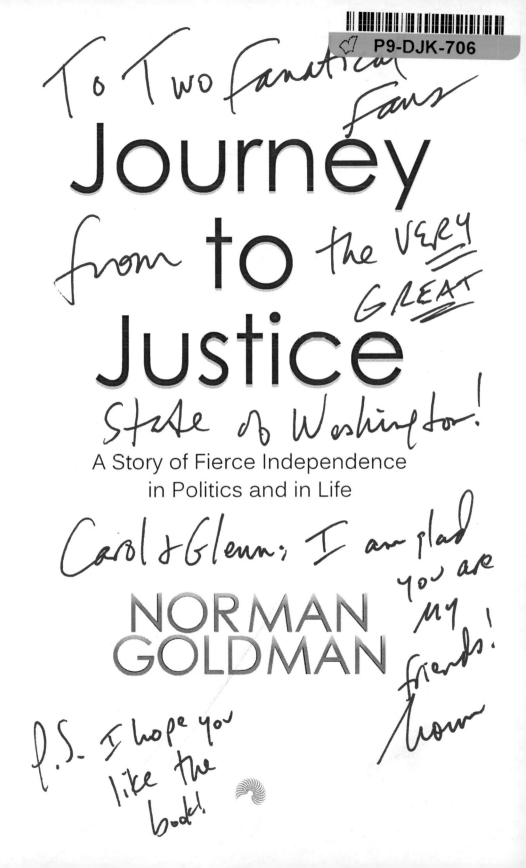

Cover and text design by Beth Farrell

Sea Script Company

Seattle, Washington

First Printing January 2012

ISBN: 978-0-9828663-6-8

Library of Congress Card Catalogue No.: 2011946086

Printed in the United States

SEA SCRIPT COMPANY
www.seascriptcompany.com
info@seascriptcompany.com
206.748.0345

CONTENTS

ACKNOWLEDGEMENTS

There are so many people to acknowledge, I could write a separate book just on *that* topic! Frances has been the love of my life for 21 years. We do so much together, it is impossible to imagine life without her. Frances' dad, Sidney, was a wonderful man and like a second father to me. We miss him a lot. My father dedicated his last years to my brothers and me. His lessons on life guide me still. In her last months, my mother must have been in agony with the knowledge that she was going to lose her husband and children while she was still young. I hope I have honored her with my life. My dad's sister Esther and her husband Joe Levy, my aunt and uncle, were role models. They showed me that money is no measure of success. Ed Schultz gave me a chance at talk radio, became my friend and mentored me when he had no reason to do so. I will always be grateful. Many people at New York University's radio station WNYU-FM (89.1 in the New York/ tri-state area) including Michael Lysak, Chris Long, Bernard Gershon, Richard Roth, Jeff Reynolds, and Steve D'Anolfo— and others too numerous to name—taught me about radio, and helped me as a high school kid to work in and fall in love with radio. Loyola Marymount University of Los Angeles, which took a chance on a penniless orphan from New York

City, and gave me a full tuition scholarship believing I could become a lawyer, I hope I have fulfilled your wishes for me. To many of the house parents in the three orphanages in which I lived, and the teachers along the way who encouraged me to not give up, to strive and work hard and who taught me so many things about life, I will always remember your kindness and try to pass it on. To my brother Allan, who struggled with life but never lost interest in the world, I hope you have found peace. Congressman Ted Weiss and his staff, especially Norma Herman, Ellen Wallach and Paula Weiss, who showed me that politics and government are a force for tremendous good in the world and can be served in honestly, deserve recognition as examples that public service is a noble calling. To President Franklin Roosevelt, whose Social Security program touched my life in so direct and meaningful a way; to the people of the City and State of New York, whose tax dollars paid for my college education; and to all the Democrats who have fought for a better world—a world of opportunity—for riffraff like me, I am so very thankful that you cared.

I could not have gotten here without each and every one of you. I have tried to carry on the fight and will never give up. There are too many other people who need the kindness of others, since we are all in this together.

· · · · ·

INTRODUCTION

I don't know what the weather was like on March 17, 1959. I suppose I could look it up, but it wouldn't matter since I wouldn't remember the day anyway. That was the day I was born in Brooklyn, New York to Max and Lillian Goldman. They say March comes in like a lion and goes out like a lamb. Since I was born in the middle of March, it makes sense that I have both lion and lamb in me. My first instinct is to be the lamb, soft and warm, rescuing animals, being friendly, working together and hoping for the best in people. You may find this hard to believe if you've spent any time with me on the radio. Life has brought out the lion in me, and the two co-exist (I hope happily) inside of me. I still try to go with the lamb first but, unfortunately and sadly too often, the lion needs to come out first, quick and roaring.

My tale is the quintessential American tale. It sounds hokey, and the story has been told many times—orphan boy makes good—but it *is* my story. I am the third of three boys, born poor and raised in very tough circumstances, who rose to make good in the world. However, unlike those who insist that we "pick ourselves up by the bootstraps" as the only way to succeed, my reality is far different; healthy doses of hard work, to be sure, but support and help at each step along the way. I am who I am because of what I have seen and what I have learned from what I have seen. I am who I am due to the opportunities I have been afforded by total strangers who had empathy for people, and not just people like me. I am who I am because of those who have helped me and those who have encouraged me. I am only here because I got help and I am not afraid to admit it. I want very much to thank and honor those who came before me and blazed the path upon which I have walked, and walk still. I now want to pass along the blessings I have received to the others who are coming up behind me. This story is for all of us, but especially for those who need a hand up along the way.

With this said, I do not believe in always turning the other cheek. I believe in responsibility and accountability. To this end, I have dubbed the other major political party the "Republicons" because they insist on calling my party the "Democrat Party," intentionally mispronouncing the name for whatever perceived advantage it has. When they whine, I tell them what I tell you here: These nasty people started it and they must be the ones to stop it. Besides, they *are* con artists; the 'Con money boys at the top con the conned at the bottom of the Republicon Party. I do not hesitate to tell a fool he is a fool. I do, however, give every fool a chance at redemption.

. . . . .

Journey to Justice

"Always obey your parents, when they are present." —Mark Twain

PART

1

HOW I GOT HERE

THE EARLY YEARS

My first memory has me in the back seat of an old sloping sedan (I called it "the root beer car" because it was the color of, well, root beer) with my mom in front, my two older brothers, one on either side of me, and my Uncle Meyer (my dad's older brother) driving. I was about three years old—1962. We were driving to the hospital to pick up my dad, who was being discharged after his second heart attack. His first was before I was born.

I recall being led, with family in tow, through a seemingly endless maze of hospital hallways. We finally emerged into a huge, open, sparsely furnished room with sunlight streaming through big windows at the far end where my father was seated on a couch in front of the windows, bathed in sunlight. He and that couch looked small, swallowed up by the size of the enormous room. I took off running toward him, and nearly killed the poor man by leaping from a distance into his arms. My mother, uncle and brothers followed and we all went home together, happy in that old root beer car. That happy moment, born of tragedy, was not to last.

Shortly thereafter, my mother was diagnosed with colon cancer. A series of hospitals, waiting rooms and visits back home was the way of life for the next two years. But I'm getting ahead of myself.

My father, Maxwell, was born on the Lower East Side of Manhattan in 1921, the fourth of five children. *His* parents were the immigrants—brought here as children from the ghettoes of Austria by *their* parents. Max's dad was born in 1892, which put my family's arrival in America around 1900. Max was a sweet and gentle man, averse to confrontation, slow to anger, smart but quiet. He was conservative and conventional in his ways. He smoked cigarettes and rarely drank, but when he did, it was beer. He wore the hats and clothes of the day. He was a big sports fan and exuded the working class ways of his upbringing. He was devoted to his family. His sisters and older brother were very close to him and each other, although Max seemed to be the glue that held them all together. His siblings had their little squabbles and backbiting with each other but about Max, they all seemed to agree, and they all adored him.

Max's mother Yetta was also born in 1892 but, like much of my family on both sides, I have scant details of her life. Yetta lived to 1955 and from everything I ever heard about her, she was a saint. She apparently had extraordinary powers, too. In her final weeks, her son-in-law Joe (my father's brother-in-law) had been attending to Yetta night and day when Yetta grabbed his face, one hand on each side, pulled him close, kissed him hard on the forehead and whispered to him, "I give you extra years." And he got them, too, although he didn't really want them since his wife (my dad's sister) died before him and he was very lonely.

Yetta made bathtub gin during the Depression, which was common in those Prohibition days. And she'd buy a chicken and manage to feed the entire tenement building they lived in there on the Lower East Side. A loaf of bread and fishes it wasn't, but I heard many stories of how selfless and wonderful my grandmother Yetta was.

My mother's side of the family is a bigger mystery than my father's side. My mother Lillian, born in 1918, was also one of five children—all born in the United States—but I never got the order correctly. My mom's parents were immigrants from Poland and that's about all I know, other than that her parents came to America around the same time as my father's family, settling in Brooklyn.

Max, Lil and their siblings all had rough lives, the classic immigrant tale of coming to America in that era. They were born poor, raised poor and grew up during the Great Depression. They also knew death at early ages. Lil's brother Morris, I am told, died at 20 of a heart attack, literally working himself to death. My middle name comes from my uncle Morris. I never met any of my grandparents, and two of my mother's siblings were already gone by the time I was born. They had no Lipitor, angioplasty or even aspirin therapy in those days.

Max's father Israel—a great name, no?—died of a heart attack on Christmas Day, 1932. He was 40. Franklin Roosevelt had been elected but not yet sworn in and the Depression was on in a big way. Max was 11. Israel had been a tailor, making $3 a week in the Depression. Max's older brother (my uncle Meyer, the root beer car driver) immediately dropped out of school and went to work. Max sold pencils and apples on the street. All five kids worked and Yetta brewed her bathtub gin. It was the 1930s and the Lower East Side of Manhattan, like much of the rest of America, was a hard place to earn a living and raise a family. Max finished high school and began college at Pace in lower Manhattan, but dropped out in 1942 to enlist in World War II. He never returned to college, GI Bill notwithstanding.

To show you the progress we've made as a society: My dad was born a natural left hander. His dad beat him and forced him to switch to the right hand, believing that being left handed was a mark of the beast, or some such silliness. My dad told me that when he was very young and at a family dinner, he cursed and his dad said, "Do that again and I'll wash your mouth out with soap." Of course, the test had to be made, so the curse was uttered, the washing occurred. All the stories I ever heard of my grandfather were that he was a strict disciplinarian.

Lil and Max met on a blind date and married on October 8, 1950. She was turning 32, he was 29. It was unusual in those days to marry late. They waited a couple of years to start having kids so that by the time I came along on St. Patrick's Day 1959, Lil was 40 and Max was 37. My two older brothers, Al and Ron, were born in 1952 and 1955.

I was born into poor circumstances, but didn't know any better and considered our family middle class. For example, we would gather our old clothes and things and put them in a big barrel for Goodwill Industries. My dad explained that there were many people worse off than we were and that we should try to help them. It made perfect sense to me and I've continued his habit.

Dad was a bookkeeper and mom worked part-time in a beauty parlor (I always loved that term—as if you go in one way and come out beautiful!), but there were early signs that we weren't living in the best class or neighborhood. We lived on the third floor of a three-story walk-up apartment house, that was by then a tenement, in the East New York/Brownsville section of Brooklyn. My family moved there shortly before I was born.

From my earliest memories, our apartment in Brooklyn had been overtaken by vermin. I remember taking a bath, I couldn't have been more than four, and two huge waterbugs (that's what we called them, they were just massive cockroaches) appeared in the corner of the tub where the wall met the top of the tub. I screamed my head off and my mom came running and pulled me out of the tub. I don't know what happened to those bugs though I can guess!

When I was seven, I watched a large waterbug walk up the wall in the dining room. My dad rolled up a newspaper and tiptoed over to it. I was standing about ten feet away. Just as my dad was about to smash it, it *flew off the wall* and landed on his shoulder! My dad screamed, "AHHH!," I screamed, "AHHHH!" and even that old waterbug must have screamed "AHHH!" as it went flying away onto the floor and was squashed by my dad's shoe. I said, "Those things *fly*!?!? Let's get out of here!" I suspect my dad was thinking the same thoughts.

The waterbugs were everywhere, and we also had rats. We had rat traps throughout the apartment. Often at night you would hear them go off. We caught rats on the backs of their heads (a messy sight no kid should see), in their mid-backs (my dad was pretty good at cleaning up these messes), and one night, a trap caught one by the tail. You could hear the "snap" of the trap clearly in the still night. We all got up and saw the rat squirming. My dad picked up the trap with the dangling rat, and we all walked into the bathroom where he dropped it—trap and all—into the bathtub and turned on the hot water. Then the four of us (this was after my mom died) watched the rat drown. While I was no fan of rodents, I felt badly for the rat and sadistic watching it. At that point—age six or so—I realized that I did not like Brooklyn and that this was no way to live.

The neighborhood was one of those ethnically homogenous areas that were so prevalent in the big cities back in those days. My earliest childhood memories of that area were of stores with signs in both English and Hebrew (or Yiddish, I could never tell the difference) and *lots* of Jewish people, especially old or what *looked* like old to my little kid eyes. By the time we moved out when I was eight, the neighborhood had "turned," meaning it became a black area, and the infamous "white flight" had occurred. As far as I could tell, we were the last white people there. The Balabans, who lived around the corner, had moved away a few months before.

It's funny how different people react to the same circumstances. In my last years there, my two best friends were black and Puerto Rican—Calvin and Anibal (nickname "Neebie" for reasons I never understood). We were inseparable and always playing ball or "ringoleevio" (a form of hide and seek, spread over an area as large as a neighborhood) or just hanging out on stoops (there were brownstones all over the area) and talking.

My oldest brother developed a strong racist streak and my father didn't react well to the influx of blacks either. During that time, when I was between five and eight, I had dinner at Calvin's and Neebie's homes and they would come over to ours. I learned early on that people are just people. I couldn't understand the racist comments of my father and oldest brother since I *knew* from personal experience that everyone I knew was just like me. But I was well aware of the racial tensions. Remember, this was Brooklyn, New York in the middle 1960s and the times they were a'changing, as Bob Dylan said.

My brothers and I were regularly mugged, sometimes violently. One spring day, we were playing ball in the schoolyard around the corner from our apartment. Late that afternoon, as

6

we were walking home with our baseball gloves under our arms, a group of black teens came running up behind us and stole our gloves. I stood there, stunned. My brother Ron ran a short distance after them and stopped. Al chased after them, only to be given a real beating when he caught up with them. When we got home, Dad was angry and yelled at us for letting it happen.

Around that same time, on a bright, sunny afternoon, I was looking down onto the street from the front windows of our apartment, and saw my two brothers being mugged at knife point. I called to my dad. He came over, leaned out the window and let loose a stream of words I didn't recall ever hearing before. He was angry! The black muggers took off and my brothers came running upstairs.

I was often mugged, usually on the subways, which was my transportation for getting around New York City. In contrast to today, the muggers of that era were more polite, less violent and certainly not as well armed. Today guns are everywhere, and murders and shootings happen all too often. In those days, muggings were done at knife point, and the muggers just wanted money. Once they got it, they were gone. Back then, my brothers and I traveled all over the city unaccompanied by an adult. I often traveled myself, alone, which would never be allowed to happen today. We thought nothing of it; the muggings were just part of the equation. By then, I realized we were poor or pretty darn close to it.

When I was about 12, living in an orphanage by then, I was on the GG train in Brooklyn near the Hoyt-Schermerhorn station (not the best part of town), and found myself alone in one of the cars. A group of young black men came into the car, walked up to me, surrounded me, and one of them took out a knife. The knife-holder said, "Give me your money," so I took out my wallet. I said, "Fellas, look, I have two dollars in my wallet and a subway token in my pocket. I need the subway token to get home, so if you'll just take the two dollars (and I showed them the open wallet with the two bills in there), I would appreciate it." They looked at each other, nodded to each other, the leader took the wallet and they left. No violence and pretty reasonable muggers, given that they could have done some serious harm. And I still had my subway token. My negotiation skills were off to a flying start!

During that time, I was well aware of my bad circumstances. As I looked back, even from the vantage point of age 12, I realized things had not been good from the beginning.

My mother died three days after I turned five. Ever since that day, at every birthday, I always know that three days later is a sad anniversary. It's just one of those things. The memories of my mom are a disorganized group of distinct events. There are a couple of dozen of these random memories. I *do* remember her and that is a good thing. She was a very devoted mother, doting on her kids in an old-fashioned way. She used to prepare different dinners for us, which drove my dad crazy. He insisted we all have one dinner, but mom was a spoiler and she did what she pleased.

She was especially close to my oldest brother Al. He was a "Mama's Boy," smothered with Mom's affection and attention. It may have been because Al was her first child and because she became a parent so late, or it may just have been her way. No matter, she kept Al close to her. Her death hit him hard. For the next six years, he fought with our father endlessly. Their bitterness toward each other was a key feature of our household.

My mom wanted a girl *real* badly, so much so that her second child was to be Veronica, but he came out as Ronald.

By the time I came along, I was to have been a girl named Norma, but in those days there was no amniocentesis or gender testing, so a child's sex was discovered the old way, upon arrival. When I emerged, my dad had the easy answer for my name—Norma became Norman. Fortunately for me, I learned the "Mom wanted a girl real bad" story later in life, and I never knew or felt any disappointment from her. She never dressed me as a girl or had me carry purses or the like, so I was spared spending money on psychiatric treatment for gender confusion.

I knew my mom as a very feminine presence. She worked in the beauty parlor and had hand creams and perfumes around the house. I remember she used Pond's cream. Whenever I see a jar of Pond's now, I think of my mother.

One night, I couldn't have been more than three and still sleeping in a crib in my parent's room, when I heard a crinkling sound. I woke up and saw a huge panda bear wrapped in cellophane being propped up on the bureau (because it was Brooklyn, we called it a "chestadraws") and nearly jumped out of my crib! My mom had intended for me to see it in the morning, but my parents made too much of a racket and woke me up so I got it that night. Years later, Dad told me he didn't want to buy the bear, it was expensive, but mom made him do it. I'm glad she did. I named him "Teddy" and he was with me until I was ten, when he couldn't take any more repairs and simply had to be thrown away. I was sad for a long time after that, having lost a friend.

I remember my mom was taking me to the dentist one sunny afternoon. She seemed healthy, so I had to have been no more than four. We passed a building around the corner from our apartment, one that I had noticed a lot before that day. I can still picture it—a long, low, brick building, painted an orange-cream monotone drab color. The Venetian blinds were always drawn shut; I could never see inside. I hardly ever saw anyone go in or out, and the whole place had an air of depression and foreboding. I asked my mom what the building was, and she said it was an "orphanage." Not knowing what that was, I asked her, and she told me. It sounded awful. I remember thinking to myself, "I'm glad I'll never be in a place like that." And I wasn't, not for another seven years.

My mom had been in and out of the hospital but was home when President Kennedy was assassinated. November 22, 1963 was four months before she died. I remember her ironing, watching soap operas on our old black and white TV. The news broke into the show and my mom started crying. I didn't know what was happening, but from the TV and her reaction, I knew it was big, major and bad. As the tragic story unfolded that day and the days thereafter, I realized that the world outside my little life was full of action, that the world was a big and active place. I was determined to explore it.

While most kids watched cartoons (and certainly I watched some, *Superman* reruns were big with me), I spent a lot of time watching reruns of *Biography* with Mike Wallace, which were filmed in the late 1950s. It was an unusual choice of program for a little kid, but I was curious about the world and this seemed a good way to get information about it. I didn't know who Mahatma Gandhi, Amelia Earhart, and Winston Churchill were, but I was finding out.

I also did a lot of reading including the usual kid stuff (I loved *Puss 'N Boots!*), but there was always a newspaper lying around for me to read, too. The paper was the *New York Daily News*, "New York's Picture Newspaper," which was not high brow stuff like *The New York Times* (which I would switch to later) but for a five, six or seven year old kid, it was plenty. *New York Daily News* was my dad's paper, a tabloid, and he would read it Hebrew style, right to left beginning with sports. For a long time, I thought the sports section *was* the front page! Whatever I could use to learn stuff, I was using— newspapers, books, TV—I was voraciously trying to explore the big, complex, mysterious world outside that always seemed to have some big crisis or strange event occurring.

I remember my parents as very close. I have no memories of them arguing, other than one or two snippy words here and there, like when my dad farted once, loudly, and my mom got annoyed and said, "That's what bathrooms are for," and we all had a good laugh. I remember them going out; they would come home late and seemed very happy together. There was an air in the house of closeness, familiarity, comfort and ease. I felt a lot of love in the house; I never felt tension or anger. Despite the poverty, of which I was mostly unaware when my mom was still alive, all seemed very nice. I had my older brothers, who were generally good to me, and my parents.

I never went to kindergarten, instead I was sent to the Pitkin Avenue Day Nursery on Pitkin Avenue in Brooklyn. This was when my mom was getting more sick, as we had housekeepers by then (more on that a bit later). My dad dropped me off in the morning, the housekeepers would pick me up in the afternoon and we would take the bus home. During my time at the Pitkin Avenue Day Nursery I learned three things: First, I hated beets; second, I played well with the other children; and third, the teachers liked me, making me very popular with everyone.

I was often sick as a child. I had it all: mumps, measles, German measles, chicken pox, pneumonia. During these illnesses, I was stuck at home in bed. In the fall of 1963, my mom was home from the hospital, and my teacher from the Pitkin Avenue Day Nursery came to our apartment with a big "Get Well" card made by my classmates and teacher. I was not only feeling sick, but I was (believe it or not) shy and did not want to come out to see the teacher. My mom came into the bedroom and said, "You don't understand, this is very unusual to have a teacher come visit with a big card from your classmates. It means you're special and popular. And besides, it's rude not to come out when someone has come to pay you a visit." So I climbed out of bed, went out to the living room, kept my head down staring at the floor, did a few stammering "Thank you's" and skedaddled back to bed as fast as I could!

I slowly came to the realization that my mom was sick and getting sicker. Things started changing. My mom was absent for longer and longer stretches. We would go to visit her in hospitals. She was always, seemingly, in a different place. One was Sloan-Kettering Cancer Institute in Manhattan. That is where they did her colon cancer surgery. After the surgery, they attached a colostomy bag to her side. Despite trying to keep me from seeing it, I saw it once, and it was a weird thing for a four year-old to see. I asked my eldest brother Al about it and he explained what it was. It didn't sound like a good thing.

This being 1963, medicine and the times were different. The doctors couldn't do much for her, and she deteriorated. My dad and I visited her once in a little red brick hospital not far from our apartment in Brooklyn. She waved out the window from her third floor room, and that was our visit. In retrospect, I realize my dad (and likely my mom, too) was trying to shield me from what was happening.

Toward the end of her life, she was brought home in a wheelchair. Since we lived on the third floor in a three-story walk-up, her wheelchair was carried by two strong young men. I was shocked to see her condition that day. Although she had just turned 45, she looked awful—totally gray hair, frighteningly emaciated, very pale, just plain bad. That was the last time I saw her, and all I remember is how she looked, not the visit itself. Not the best way to have a final visit with your mother, but that's the way it went.

My mom had been out of the house for what seemed like a long time and, since each of my brothers had their own room and I was still little, I slept in the big king bed with my dad, with me in the middle and my panda bear on my mom's side of the bed.

It was either the night she died (March 20, 1964) or a night very shortly thereafter, I woke up in the middle of the night with my pillow all wet. I hadn't wet the bed for a long time and was startled at the water on the pillow. I started feeling around "down there" to see what I had done. To my surprise, the bed was dry and I was still wondering where that water had come from. It was then I looked over and saw my dad crying in his sleep; I think in his sleep. The tears were really flowing and I can still see the anguish on his face. I was frozen, stock still. I didn't know what to do. I didn't want to wake him or disturb him, but I really didn't know *what* to do, so I did nothing. Just laid there, frozen, watching him cry. He finally quieted down and I managed to fall back asleep. I never told him about it, but I watched him a long time that night, just thinking about how much pain the poor man was in, and how much he missed my mom. It was an odd way to bond with one's father, but it sure showed me the human being he was and that even adults were capable of tears and pain and vulnerability. All quite a powerful lesson for a kid at age five years and three or so days.

I didn't attend my mom's funeral. My eight-year-old brother Ron and I were left at home. Again, to "protect" us from this painful experience. Though I don't recall it, my dad's siblings told me years later that my dad was a real mess during my mom's illness. He was distracted, deluged with bills, didn't make much money, almost lost his driver's license from all the traffic tickets, and was not well himself, already having had two heart attacks. To help pay for my mom's funeral, my dad had to sell things: the sewing machine, my mom's clothes, the piano. That piano is an interesting thing—my parents forced my oldest brother Al to take lessons and he hated it! He fought like mad to avoid it. I, on the other hand, wanted very much to learn to play. My parents finally gave up on Al and the piano. I never said, "Hey, give *me* those lessons if Al doesn't want them," which taught me a valuable lesson, "Don't ask, don't get." It was a lesson I applied often as I got older. The irony is that, to this day, I still haven't learned to play the piano even though we have one in the house. It's simply a function of time—there's never enough. Maybe one day.

Much of my life in the months after my mother died I was what we now call a "Latch Key Kid." I was home alone during the day, unsupervised. Usually this was not a problem. For the most part, I minded my manners and watched my own version of educational TV (Hitler scared me even then—Mike Wallace sure portrayed him as a monster!) and read stuff. But I was very lonely and missed my dad terribly and hounded him with phone calls at work. He told me I had to stop and eventually put a lock on the phone to keep me from calling, it was affecting his job. I got around that by simply taking the handset off the hook and clicking the hook repeatedly until an operator came on. My brother Al had quietly told me how to do it—he was clever.

I eventually did leave the poor man alone at work except during that time I almost burned the house down which, given the rats and roaches, may have been an improvement. Joking aside, I was playing with matches (don't try this at home, especially at age five or six) and paper towels—a very bad combination—when the wad of paper caught fire like a fireball. I threw the flaming wad out the window. It went down a large, pentagon shaped airshaft enclosed on all sides by the walls of the building and open at the top. There was a ton of debris at the bottom (remember, we were three flights up) so I craned my neck to see if the debris had caught fire. I had visions of flames lapping up the sides of the building, and freaked out. Another call to my dad and in a couple of minutes it seemed the entire New York City Fire Department was in the apartment, pouring *lots* of water out the window through *really* big hoses. Disaster averted, but I sure learned a valuable lesson about playing with fire. My dad was not amused.

I realize now these acts were all cries for attention and help. Fortunately, no other calamities occurred and I made my way forward a somewhat calmer and less dangerous child.

While my dad didn't earn much, he did have a steady job that he enjoyed. He was a bookkeeper for Arrow Conduit, a construction materials supply company. Conduit is tubing that encases wires and such, and my dad was the bookkeeper for the company for a long time. He was very popular there and they were very supportive. So despite the troubles he was having, at least he had a stable job and friends at work. This, as it turned out later, would be the last pillar of support that, once withdrawn, would prove to be his end.

After my mom's death, Dad received about $100 a month in Social Security survivor's benefits for his three sons—about $33 a month for each of us. While this may not sound like much, in the early and mid-1960s it was helpful, especially to a widower making about $100 a week at his job and having three young boys to support. Franklin Roosevelt was already touching my life! That $100 a month paid the rent on our rat and roach infested six-room-cold-water railroad flat. But Dad knew it was time to go.

One sad truth about my dad was that, before I was born, our family was living in a New York City Housing Authority project in Brooklyn. We were kicked out because Dad was making money on the side moonlighting at a part-time bookkeeping job and *not* reporting that income to the Housing Authority. That made us ineligible for public housing and we had to move, which is how we ended up in the place I first called home with the rats and roaches.

After my mom died, Dad reapplied to get back into public housing. They put him through the ringer (as well they should considering he burned them once by being dishonest), which is why it took us three years to get back into public housing. I'm sure my dad felt guilty about the whole thing for the rest of his life. He always taught me that honesty was the best policy. He learned the hard way to remind himself of that.

* * * * *

2
THE PROJECTS

We finally did move to a public housing project in Flushing, Queens. (There's an old joke, "Flushing Queens? I'd love to.") To us it seemed like heaven. No bugs, no rats, actual grass patches to throw a football around. As far as I knew, it was the middle class.

We moved on June 30, 1967. I was eight. My mom had already been gone more than three years. It was a gray, warm and rainy day in New York. We had already visited the apartment we were going to move to—a small two bedroom, one bath unit on the sixth floor of a seven-story building. We were all excited, I think my dad most of all. There was a big moving van for our furniture. As we led the way from Brooklyn to Queens, it seemed like another world. The housing project, called "Pomonok" (a Native name, of course), had been built in the early and mid-1950s and so wasn't very old. It was also very well cared for—there were well-manicured expanses of grass and various playgrounds. The project itself was very large with many buildings spread over a huge group of square and rectangular blocks with pathways and walkways winding through the development. Directly across from our building was a large new shopping center. A big supermarket was there; a coffee shop, a candy store and various other stores were all a moment away. Very easy access to shopping! Years later, when I worked for Congressman Weiss and did "constituent service" (focusing on housing issues), I worked closely with the New York City Housing Authority and some of its higher-up bureaucrats. I became friendly with one older man and told him of my experiences. When I mentioned Pomonok, he said it was "the crown jewel" of their system—the most desirable of the properties. That was certainly true compared to what we had just left. I was convinced we had ascended into the middle class.

I was starting third grade that September of 1967, and the public school I was to attend was a short walk away. I was able to come home for lunch. There was an area of undeveloped woods on the way, diagonally across from our building. It was always nice to look into the woods and see trees and hear birds. Years later when I returned, those woods were gone, developed into a police station and other buildings.

On the first day of third grade at my new school there in Flushing, my dad dropped me off on his way to work. I was standing there on this big concrete school yard with all the kids lined up behind signs for their classes. I found mine, but an overwhelming sense of loneliness and sadness came over me. My dad had just driven away, I knew no one, and I felt swallowed up in an ocean of unknown kids and adults. I started to cry. One of the other kids went and got my new teacher and she came over and was very nice and comforting and helped calm me down. She was very kind. That simple act of kindness has always stayed with me reminding me that we each have within us the power to comfort each other, if only we would try. I went on to make lots of friends and learned a valuable lesson: Adapting is part of life and what is once new and strange soon becomes old and familiar.

From the time my mom was first sick, housekeepers began appearing at our home. From 1964 to 1970, there was always a housekeeper present from mid-morning to dinnertime. And we had many. They came and went, sometimes one housekeeper a week. Of all the housekeepers we had, two were wonderful. Thankfully, one was around at the time around my mother's death and the other around the time of my father's death. I still remember their names and their faces. Mrs. Goldsmith was a black lady who seemed straight out of Central Casting— heavy-set, jovial, smiling, a dead ringer for the actress Hattie McDaniel. She was as kind and sweet as any person I've ever known and was the glue that kept us together during those sad days of my mother's death. She cooked, cleaned, made sure we did our homework, and looked after us with as much love and fussing as any mother would look after her own kids.

At the time of my father's decline and death, we had Mrs. Brown, a short, thin black lady with wiry hair and a stern but gentle manner. She was efficient and could scold, but never with harshness or ill feeling. Like Mrs. Goldsmith, she kept our household together as my dad sank towards his death in 1970. In between these two wonderful women was a blur of women—white, black, Hispanic, all short-termers. The reason was largely that my brothers and I drove them crazy! Mrs. Goldsmith and Mrs. Brown had tremendous empathy for what they knew was happening in our home. They had families of their own and went far beyond the call of duty to help us through the tough times we were experiencing. They put up with, and indeed, mastered the chaos of our home. They earned our respect and love and were able to get some level of control over us. The others, not so much. We were vibrant kids, bursting with energy that made our household stand on its ear. The other housekeepers just wanted to do their jobs and get out—and that is what they did.

The housekeepers, as I learned later, were employed by The Jewish Family Service, a charitable organization still very much in existence today and doing the good work of helping people in need. Not exclusive to helping Jewish people (the name is a legacy from many years ago), the JFS supplied these housekeepers and paid most of their salary. My dad paid something like $20 per week. The goal, of course, was to help keep the family together. This effort, to help keep our family together, is one more example of how none of us can make it on our own. The housekeepers would cook dinner as their last chore of the day. My brothers and I would eat together early and Dad's dinner was waiting for him, warming in the oven, when he got home from work.

Those Pomonok years were ones of special closeness for my brothers and me. We would listen to the radio with dinner and it was *always* set to Music Radio WABC—77 AM on your dial. Those were the days of "Cousin Brucie," Harry Harrison, Dan Ingram and the legendary cast of DJs on the top station in New York. There was no FM to speak of in those days—AM was king and everybody was listening. When I was a little kid in Brooklyn, we listened to "The Good Guys" of WMCA 570 AM. Those two radio stations, playing the hot top-40 hits of the day, defined my childhood. My dad played them in the car and we listened to them at home. I was always mesmerized by how they made all that sound come out of that little box. As a little kid, I envisioned tiny little people and bands inside the radio, all making music. My brothers laughed at me when I told them that, and explained it had to do with invisible waves coming through the air and into the box. Whatever it was, I was sold. I wondered what all those people talking out of the radio looked like, and I sure wanted to be one of the ones on the other end of that box. My love of radio started early and has never waned.

We spent three years in the Pomonok housing project. For me and my brother Ron, it was from June 30, 1967 to September 10, 1070. Those first two and a half years, until the end of 1969, were the happiest years of my childhood, beyond any doubt. My oldest brother Al had a different experience and I'll get there in a moment. I spent the third, fourth and fifth grades in Pomonok, although the last year (fifth grade) was very rocky. The public school I attended was modern and clean. My brothers and I were very popular at Pomonok and there were lots of young families with kids our ages in the area. We were always playing sports—baseball and football, mostly, but whatever could be done, we did. Sledding was abundant as there were little hills right behind our building. Hide and seek or whatever else could be done, we did.

I was in Little League and my dad was our manager. My oldest brother Al played Pop Warner football—he was the right guard on a dreadful team, but our dad was one of the "chain gangs" who moved the ten-yard markers on the side of the field. One day, a running play, a sweep, led to a pile up out of bounds, and our dad was under the pile! I saw it happen from the other side line—one second he was there and then he was gone. I was horrified, thinking my dad was dead, but he emerged relatively unscathed and we all breathed a sigh of relief.

Despite not having much money, Dad found the cash to take us to Mets games where we would sit way far upstairs in the general admission seats, and then sneak down in the later innings to better seats. Shea Stadium was not far from our house and when the Mets were home at night, we could see the glow of the lights from our living room windows. We would watch baseball, football, hockey and basketball on TV, and Dad taught us the games and the rules. Occasionally, we would troop down to Madison Square Garden to see the Rangers play hockey or the Knicks play basketball, but baseball and football were my sports although I did enjoy watching the Boston Celtics on TV. Those were the days of John Havlicek and Jo Jo White, and I still can hear the squeaking of their sneakers on that parquet floor at the old Boston Garden.

I was good at baseball. Mostly a pitcher, I pitched a one-hitter in Little League with the only hit being an error by the second baseman letting a little pop fly fall behind him. Called a hit by the official scorer, my dad and I declared it a no-hitter and I even got a little story in the local newspaper, which my dad stayed up late into the evening typing on an old typewriter to submit to the newspaper, the *Long Island Press*. What a guy! I knew my dad had been a pitcher himself (he was a lefty, me a righty, irony of ironies!) in the Central Park leagues when he was a kid, so it must have given him great satisfaction watching his sons play ball, too.

I realize now how much he was sacrificing. He was raising his three boys with never a day off. Even weekends he had us around him, usually with sports as the bond, but he was always *involved* in our lives. His relaxation came at night. After dinner, he and I would watch TV and after I went to bed, he would watch more TV and finish the evening reading the newspaper at the dining room table. On weekends, we would watch sports on TV or *do* sports and that was our life, Max and his three boys. Fortunately for my dad, he did get summers off, at least part of it. More on that in a bit.

Between 1967 and 1969, during dinners with my brothers, we always heard Howard Cosell "speaking of sports on "The American Contemporary Radio" at 5:25 each afternoon. We would all practice our Howard impersonations, which was the first impersonation I ever did! Dad would come home around 6:00. Having had our dinner earlier, we would be doing our homework while he ate dinner. Then at 7:00, I would sit with him and watch *The CBS Evening News with Walter Cronkite*. It was usually just the two of us, my brothers were not particularly interested and would go out or do things in their room. I really loved that time watching the news with my father and felt he enjoyed having me with him. He would patiently answer my questions and seemed to be happy that I was interested. Remember that these were extraordinarily turbulent times: Vietnam was raging; the Six Day War in the Middle East had just taken place; Martin Luther King and Robert Kennedy were assassinated; the 1968 Democratic National Convention in Chicago was a made-for-TV reality show. There was plenty in the news every night and I was *hooked*. With my dad there to guide me, I became a news junkie very early on.

My dad always encouraged me to read and I continued to read voraciously. Dad read to me a lot when I was little and he would trick me into reading as I got older. I always wanted to stay up later than my bedtime because my brothers did, so my dad would tell me, "OK, if you go to bed and read for a half-hour, you can come out and watch the news with me." Most nights I read longer than 30 minutes and fell asleep in bed. However, a few times I did manage to make it out to the living room to watch some TV.

I excelled in school, especially those years in Pomonok. I learned quickly. I liked my teachers and they liked me and I had lots of friends. My dad seemed happy, my brothers and I settled into a nice life (certainly nicer than the hot and cold running rats and roaches of Brooklyn) and things were brightening up. From June 1967 to the end of 1969, my brothers and I were closer than we had been (and we had always been pretty close). During that short window of time, things seemed good. Not perfect, mind you, but good. I don't want to paint an overly rosy picture of the times, there were problems, but nothing out of the ordinary. We had housekeepers coming and going, but the household ran relatively smoothly. We all, our father included, developed a routine, a rhythm, that seemed to work for us all, and the stability was appreciated.

Around that time, I was eight or nine, I was doing my homework and there was a map of the United States as a centerfold in my book (Hugh Hefner had *nothing* on my social studies book). I studied it for a good long while. Then I carried it out to my dad, seated at the dining room table. I laid the centerfold before him and started pointing, "Look, here is Utah, here is California, here is Nebraska and Texas and Alabama and all these far off places. Here is New York" (pointing to a little dot on the map). "I've seen New York, and it's bad. Let's go see these other places and move there." He said, "But this is our home. This is where I was born, you were born here, our family is here. We have history here. My parents came here as kids. This is our home." I thought about it a long second and realized that what I wanted to say was probably better left unsaid. What I was thinking was, "This is your home, pal, it's got nothing for me. First chance I get, I'm outta here." Wisdom and avoiding a swift smack to the chops won out and I silently carried that book back to my bed, but that thought of fleeing the urban nightmare never left.

My brother Al and my dad had a very rocky relationship. They were constantly fighting and, one day, nearly came to blows. Al had a baseball bat and Dad had a chair. Ron and I jumped in and grabbed them and kept them from clobbering each other. The source of the friction, from what I could tell, was that my dad was very disappointed in Al and vice versa. Al, sad to say, was kind of odd (I've come to believe he had Asperger's Syndrome, a form of high functioning autism). He was very heavy, he dressed oddly, behaved unusually (he did repetitive motions and had strange, obsessive/compulsive habits) and spoke his mind—sometimes to hurtful ends. He liked to taunt my father, denouncing Judaism and eating with his left hand, which drove my dad crazy, as you can tell from the story of my dad's own experience with left-handedness. To a certain extent, it was typical teenage/parent conflict. On the other hand, it was the absence of our mother and because my dad picked on Al to try to get him to behave more, well, more normally. Several times I remember seeing a look on my dad's face when he and Al were fighting. The look was a combination of exasperation, bewilderment and frustration topped with anger. I could almost read his mind, "I made this kid. I saw him born and grow. How in God's name could this have happened right under my nose?"

I mentioned the Jewish Family Service awhile back, and the subsidized housekeepers. One of the other things about being with the Jewish Family Service was social workers. I became all too well acquainted with them throughout my youth and finally concluded, when I was an adult, that social workers are not bad people. But it was the *type* of social worker I was subjected to as a child that gave me a bad opinion of them at the time. During the days of my mother's decline and death, my brother Al would see social workers. I never really knew what he and they discussed, but I intuited that it was some sort of "therapy." What "therapy" was I did not know, but since I didn't have to participate, I didn't give it much thought. After my mother's death, once a month, my father would trundle us all into the car and drive us to Manhattan where we would sit for an hour or so with a social worker. I never spoke much (a trait I was soon to break forever) but observed that most of the time was spent by my father and oldest brother discussing what was on their minds and their feelings. Again, most of this did not mean much to me and I never really gave it much thought, except when my father was near surrendering custody of us (and near death, as it turned out) in the summer of 1970.

It was a couple of weeks before I was sent to the first orphanage, and a social worker had the four of us in a room at the office in Manhattan. By then, my dad was in pretty bad shape: thin, listless, a ghost of his former self. The social worker was asking him how he felt about giving up his kids. He broke down and started crying, and I got angry. It seemed to me this was torture. I mean, who *wouldn't* feel terrible about having to give up his kids? I didn't say anything, and certainly should have, but decided then and there I did not like social workers or "therapy." These types of social workers, I learned later, fancied themselves latter day Sigmund Freuds. Armed with little more than a Master's Degree and a few hours "clinical training," they believed they were psychoanalysts *par excellence*. Later, when I tried to tell them otherwise, they reacted rather negatively—imagine that.

In late 1969, Al got a job at the Post Office working part time in the Grand Central Station building. He had turned 17 and was making very good money for his age. He was a senior at Stuyvesant High School on the Lower East Side of Manhattan. Dad would drive him to the subway station on the way to work (heaven only knows *what* they talked about on those rides), and Al would go to work after school, returning late at night. We didn't see much of him. By the end of 1969, things changed in our home, and changed dramatically for the worse.

The company my dad worked for, Arrow Conduit, was moving from its location in New York to Long Island, many miles away, too far for my dad to commute. He had to get another job. They helped him get another job as a bookkeeper in Long Island City, just on the Queens side of the East River, directly across from Manhattan. I don't know much of the details, but my dad didn't like the job. His co-workers or boss (or both) didn't like him either so that job didn't last long. He left it in January 1970. Whether he was fired or quit is something I'll never know. It was the last time he would ever work again. I noticed a quick and decided shift in my dad's attitude. He suddenly seemed to lose energy; he lost interest in things. He applied for and received unemployment insurance, but he became listless. He wouldn't eat and seemed distant, distracted and disinterested. In short, he was very depressed.

He slid further into this depression throughout January and into February. Then he had another heart attack. My brothers and I were eating dinner. It was a cold, rainy, raw February evening when we got a phone call from our Aunt Ethel, one of my dad's sisters, who lived nearby. She told us to get ready; she and her husband were coming to pick us up. We were driven over to Queens General Hospital where my dad was in the Intensive Care Unit. I couldn't get too close to him; they kept us outside the ward (it was a very large room), but I could see him. He was in one of the first beds in the room near the doors; I managed to park myself right outside the big double doors of the ward. He was in some sort of *very* fitful sleep and was violently thrashing around in bed, letting out these blood curdling, loud moans and cries that sent shivers down my spine and made my blood run cold. Between the writhing in bed and those other-worldly sounds emitted every half minute or so, I was in a cold sweat and scared out of my wits. It didn't take a scientist to realize he was in trouble. I looked at my brothers standing nearby, and they were white as sheets themselves. It was a month before my eleventh birthday, our mother had been gone six years and I was feeling very afraid.

Dad gradually recovered some strength over the next few days, and I was able to visit him. In one of those visits, I got a political lesson. A young man came by dressed in all whites and gave my father some pills. My dad said, "Thank you, nurse." I was startled. I said to my dad, "He's a man, only women are nurses." I had never seen a male nurse before or, for that matter, a woman doctor. My father explained that there are men and women doctors *and* nurses. Lesson learned.

I was in the fifth grade. We were still living in the housing project there in Flushing but my life was going to hell. I was having behavioral problems, my mind was wandering in school, I had no interest in doing my homework, and was withdrawn from my friends. My teacher noticed and I was sent to the school counselor. She was a nice enough lady and I would talk to her from time to time. I discovered that any time I wanted to get out of class I could just raise my hand and say, "I want to go see the counselor," and I was allowed out. I abused this little privilege finding it more interesting to wander the halls on my way to her office rather than sit in class. No doubt I was in trouble due to watching my dad's condition deteriorate.

Those months, from January to July 1970, when Ron and I were once again sent to summer camp, were very unpleasant. We were essentially fending for ourselves. We would have dinner each evening at our aunts' apartments on a rotating basis. Fortunately, our three aunts all lived nearby.

Our dad spent much of his time in the hospital psychiatric ward. The last housekeeper we had, Mrs. Brown, one of the two good ones, was there and did what she could, but we were all in a state of fear and despair. It's not good to have three young boys (two teens and a pre-teen) living basically unsupervised. Homework went undone, personal hygiene habits went untended, irregular hours were kept, necessary new clothes went unbought, discipline disappeared. We struggled through those months until the school year ended, then we were off to camp again—at least Ron and I were off to camp, Al was in for a very bad summer.

Every summer after my mom died, my dad would send us to summer camp, usually for the whole summer. I figured out later this gave him a break—less responsibility for him and a chance to not be burdened with three young boys. The grind of being on duty as a single father seven days a week year-round would be rough on anyone. For a man with a weak heart, an empty wallet and sadness from losing his love, the burden was no doubt very heavy. For me, the first year of summer camp was a horrible experience. I was five or six and the time away was torture. I believe that first stint was for three weeks although it seemed like three years. My camp counselor was verbally abusive (at least he was not physically abusive), and I was constantly crying and begging to go home. My brothers were also there though in different areas of the camp. I would find them and beg them to get me home only to be crushed when they told me they were powerless to help. I concluded that it is not a good idea to send a five or six year-old away from home for an extended (or really any) period of time.

I managed to survive that summer camp experience and found that, as the years passed, the camps got more enjoyable. One thing I *did* learn at camp, and learned repeatedly, was that

I hated asphalt and the city and loved nature. I realized that cockroaches and rats are *urban* wildlife—rabbits, raccoons, deer and the like were *real* nature! I loved swimming in clear lakes. I loved the coolness of the mountains in summer. I loved the fresh air and handling snakes in "nature shop" and walking in the woods. I *really* loved walking in the woods. The more foliage the better! I juxtaposed my summers in the mountains with life in the city with its air pollution and humidity and stifling heat reflecting off old, dirty concrete. I remembered the horrible subways—noisy, dirty and dangerous. I looked at the pitiful trees growing (if you could call it that) out of squares cut in the sidewalks and I thought, "This city life sucks."

Being that we were poor, the camps we attended were either "charity" camps or regular camps where we were the charity cases. One camp had us arrive with nothing except a toothbrush; they supplied the clothes and all. The problem was the clothes were awful—*you* try wearing girls' underwear! I just tore them to shreds and did my best, such are the indignities of poverty. One summer we were bused back to the city, as usual, at the end of camp in August. When we were dropped off, it was a horrible day—the heat and humidity off the charts; the smoke and air pollution was terrible. It was so hot, my sneakers actually started to melt into the asphalt! My dad was there to get me, and I told him, "Send me back, I like camp better than the city!" I'm very glad for the experience charity provided; proof that no one is self-made. We should each try to help out our fellows to the best of our ability.

After my mom died and I was about six, my dad piled my brothers and me and my Uncle Joe (my dad's brother-in-law, his sister Esther's husband, who got the extra years from my grandmother) into his big 1959 Chevy Belair, and we went to Cooperstown, New York to visit the Baseball Hall of Fame.

We stayed in a place called "Howe Caverns" which were free-standing bungalows near the Hall of Fame. (They're still there—I checked!) We all stayed in the one bungalow. It was crowded, but there was an extra room in the back, walled off from the main room with a sliding glass door. The back room itself was a sunroom. It looked out onto a beautiful ravine. I fell in love with that sunroom. I can still see it in my mind's eye, so peaceful and pretty, the antithesis of the city. My brothers and I played cards in there, but I just wanted to look out at the scenery. I realized I liked the country better than the city and even though I now live in Los Angeles, the area where I live has trees and wildlife and some semblance of peace and quiet. It's close enough to country living to justify all the city amenities I have come to enjoy like major league baseball and L.A. Kings hockey games!

The last summer of my dad's life, the summer of 1970, found my brother Ron and I at another summer camp for the whole summer. Fortunately, we were able to bring our own clothes this time. It was a regular camp and we were the charity cases. By that summer, Al was about to turn 18 and my dad was continuing his steady decline. My Uncle Meyer was spending a lot of time at our place in the Pomonok projects helping to look after my dad. The stories I heard later from Al were deeply disheartening and sorrowful. There was a role reversal: Al became the dad and Dad became the kid. This was especially strange for Al, given all the fighting and acrimony the two of them had inflicted upon each other for the past six years. I can only imagine how my dad felt about it. Al would constantly have to nag our father to take his pills. Al told me Dad would stand there rolling the pills around in his hand, endlessly just rolling them around, with this far-off look in his eyes. He had lost so much weight, his false teeth didn't fit properly anymore. His clothes hung off him, and he refused to get new ones. He let his car get repossessed. Al paid the bills. Uncle Meyer and Al could only get him to an occasional baseball game. He took no pleasure in going, he only went to satisfy them. One of his great loves in life, baseball, held no more interest for him.

I can only imagine the depths of sadness that had taken hold of my father. He was a shadow of his former self. My dad was usually described as happy-go-lucky and always smiling. But the smile had left him and, unfortunately, had left him for good. He must have missed my mother terribly. He had fought so long and given so much of himself that he was spent. I see that now; I missed seeing it then.

Late in that summer of 1970, Ron and I were summoned to the camp chief's office. He told us we were going to New York in a few days for a meeting, topic unknown. It seemed very mysterious. The camp chief had no details, at least none he was sharing with us. This was extremely unusual, which made me both very curious and very nervous. When the day came, we were driven to the local train station and left there. We got on the train for Manhattan and the conductor came along, asking for money and tickets. We had neither, so we were put off the train. I was terrified. Standing there, alone, penniless and in a strange place was a very empty feeling. I started crying and getting hysterical, "What would become of us?" Fortunately, Ron had his wits about him. He called the camp collect. They came and got us and took us back to camp. The meeting was rearranged for a few days later. Ron had just turned 15, I was 11.

When we finally did make it into New York, we met some people at the Jewish Child Care Association (J.C.C.A.). The organization has been in existence since the middle 1800s and still exists today. Despite the religious character of the name, "The Agency" as we called it, is funded by the government and, therefore, cannot discriminate on any basis. The name is a legacy. We were told that upon our return from camp at summer's end, we would be placed in "group residences" in different parts of the city; split up and sent away from home. We did not see our father on this one-day trip. We did see him upon our return. That was the meeting with the social worker who made my dad cry, asking him how he felt about giving up his kids. I later learned that my dad's sisters convinced him that he couldn't keep us; he was not fit to care for us the way he had for the past six years. I remembered what those months earlier in the year were like and did *not* want to repeat *that* experience.

Thus it came to be that my dad signed over custody of Ron and myself to the State of New York, which in turn, immediately handed us over to the J.C.C.A. I later surmised that this was the final act that killed my dad. But he had one last indignity before the end. Summer camp finished up in late August. On September 10, 1970, I was to be delivered to a "group residence" in Far Rockaway, beyond Kennedy Airport, on the far outreaches of New York City (when they say *Far* Rockaway, they ain't kidding). Ron was to be dropped off at a different group residence (for a different age group) in Rego Park, Queens, not far from where our father and Al remained at the Pomonok project in Flushing. Al escaped the entire experience. He turned 18 in September 1970, and began college at Queens College, within walking distance of our apartment in the projects.

The night before I was taken to the Far Rockaway residence, I cried a lot. I slept on the couch in the living room, perhaps because my Uncle Meyer was there and sleeping in my bed. It was better that way, anyway, since my crying wouldn't have made my dad feel any better. I was scared. I remember vowing to myself that one day I would come back, re-rent the apartment we had been in and everything would be all right again, safe, happy and warm. This thought comforted me enough to let me sleep even though I knew in the back of my mind, even then, that what I imagined would never happen.

The next day, Dad borrowed a car and drove me to the place in Far Rockaway. It was a long, quiet and sad ride. *I* was scared about what *I* was about to confront; *he* must have felt like an utter failure. I was focused on myself at the time but I realize now, he must have been wracked with overwhelming guilt. He likely felt like he let his beloved Lil down; he could not care for *their kids* anymore. He could not keep a job; he could not care for himself; he must have felt about as awful as any person can possibly feel. Just days earlier he had cried in front of us under the social worker's unfeeling questions about losing us; his manhood was being stripped from him. He probably felt like it was entirely his fault. He was probably reflecting on his life (he had just turned 49 three days before taking me and Ron to our new homes) and whipping himself for not taking advantage of the G.I. Bill; for being poor; for not providing the material comforts of life to his family. I can see now how it would all come crashing in on him. The task of carrying his own kids to their new homes had to be the final straw—the final declaration of his failure as a father.

All these years I've felt this overwhelming sense of sadness for what my dad went through. I would give anything to see him again, just for a minute, to tell him how much I love him and how sorry I am for all that he went through. And yes, how sorry I am for adding my measure (or more than my measure) of burden to his troubles. I can only imagine how terrible he felt having dropped his two youngest sons off at orphanages on that one day. After me, he had to go and do the same thing with Ron.

* * * * *

FAR ROCKAWAY

At the end of that long, sad ride, my dad and I arrived at a large, old but well-tended Victorian house with a porch. It was on a residential street in an older, nicely-kept neighborhood with Archie Bunker-style working class homes and leafy trees. It was a neighborhood seen in cities everywhere; nothing unusual, except that this place where I was going was not common. There was a Young Men's Hebrew Association (YMHA) next door and directly across a narrow street behind the property was Far Rockaway High School, a public school. The Victorian house, as I quickly learned, was where the administrative offices of the group residence were located and where the married couple responsible for the overall running of the place lived. There were also, in this house, small offices where social workers would meet with kids. The property itself was quite large. The actual residence for the kids was behind the house. There was a walkway on the side of the property leading to the back and a large one-story building. Next to this building was a concrete-surfaced playground with a basketball court and a small grass strip. A tall, black, wrought iron fence surrounded the entire property.

The place accommodated 20 to 22 kids—10 or 11 boys and 10 or 11 girls, depending upon need. Each of the boys' and girls' bedrooms (three each, one room for five or six kids; one for three kids; one for two kids) were on opposite ends of the building. In the middle was a very large, square room that doubled as a living room and dining room. It was an enormous room with a big brown plastic sliding divider that could be used to split the room in half. Each side of the room had a TV with old but useable chairs and sofas in front of them. The "living room" portion was on one side and the "dining room" portion was on the other. The dining room area was deeper into the room and had entrances to the large kitchen behind it. Dining room tables were of various shapes and sizes, enough to seat approximately 30 people. It turns out that the home was designed as a kosher Jewish residence. The kitchen had two sides—one for milk and one for meat. While the place was non-sectarian and kids of all races and religions were there, it was kept kosher.

After we checked in with the director of the place at the Victorian house, we were walked back to the long, low building and I was given a quick tour then shown my room, a large room shared with four other boys. Other than the enormous room that acted as combination living and dining room, there was one hall going off to the side. This is where the bedrooms and bathroom were situated. The bathroom was a community-style room: a tub was at the far end, shower stalls, sinks and toilets were along the walls. The girls' side was identical to the boys' side. They sometimes switched sides if they had more boys or girls at any given time and needed to re-configure the rooms for more or fewer of one gender or the other. There was a pay phone at either end of the living room by the hall leading to the bedrooms. We could get calls, but for outgoing calls we needed dimes and other change. This could prove embarrassing, such as when you were on a call and your time ran out. You would hear clicking and the operator would come on to say you needed to put in more money for the next few minutes. *Very* hard to explain why you were on a pay phone *at home* if you were talking to a girl, for example, and not trying to let on that your living arrangement was, shall we say, unconventional.

You started off quartered in the big bedroom and then, as "seniority" developed and kids moved on, you were able to move into the two smaller rooms with just one or two roommates. During the 18 months I lived there, I had lived in all three bedrooms with various roommates.

On that first day, my dad was there along with several of the other boys and the director of the place. They were observing the scene at close range. As I unpacked, I saw that I needed hangers. Being very uncomfortable, I whispered to my dad to bring hangers the next time he came. Some of the kids overheard and brought me hangers. I appreciated the gesture. After I unpacked, I walked with my dad to the car. As you can imagine, neither one of us was very happy. We were both in kind of a daze. I hugged and kissed him and he drove off. As I turned back to walk into the place, I knew I was in for an adventure of great uncertainty but hoped it would only be for a short time. I figured I would just play it a day at a time and that it would indeed be temporary, that my dad would get better and come back to take me home.

It was September 10th and I had four days to adjust until the next school year started. I was about to begin the sixth grade. I asked my new cohorts to give me a tour of the neighborhood and they obliged. Mostly, they were good enough kids; I got to know them slowly. The immediate neighborhood was a small and decent enclave of working to middle-class homes in a large area that was, in parts, not doing so well and in other parts was pretty nice. Poverty, public housing and abandoned cars were one-half mile away and further to one side. Nice large apartment buildings, a park with baseball diamonds and clean wide streets on the ocean were a half mile in a different direction. I took refuge there on many days, walking the beach and thinking.

In those first few weeks in "the residence," I occupied my time trying to get acclimated to my new situation. I had new friends to make, a new school to get used to, a whole new life to get into. I saw no other options so I threw myself into it. I was 11 and this was my third place to live. All in all, it could have been a lot worse—the food was edible, the school was a regular public school, I could walk there and back in about 15 minutes, the "house parents" were decent enough and my fellow cohabitants (or whatever you want to call them) seemed normal enough.

There was a kitchen staff of three or four people. They cooked, washed dishes, ordered food and made sure the place was stocked. The "house parents" stayed four days a week; usually two were on duty at a time with some overlap. There were girls' and boys' house parents. Their job was to wake us up in the morning and make sure we washed, brushed our teeth, got dressed and did our chores—cleaning the bathrooms and what not—and then make sure we did our homework and went to bed on time. They had their own apartments on the outside but also had rooms in the front house where they would stay when on duty. They were on duty 24 hours-a-day for the four days of their week. Typically the house parents were in their late 20s and in graduate school (usually for social work or psychology). While this job didn't pay a lot, meals were included and they had a place to stay so that their living arrangements off-site could be inexpensive and modest. For the most part, they cared about the kids and wanted to help. I remember many of them from all three places I ended up living. The house parents were the best part of the whole experience. Most, though not all, were very nice and easy to get along with. In Far Rockaway they would play basketball with us on the court outside the main building where we lived. They would also watch TV with us and they tried to be helpful.

I got adjusted to my new surroundings pretty quickly and got into a routine. I had no choice. School was school. I still had to go to the bathroom and shower. I still needed to eat and do homework. I got to know my fellow inhabitants and *that* was a fascinating discovery. I discovered quickly that most of the kids in the place had *four live parents*—two birth parents who had divorced and then two step parents after their natural parents had remarried. And I discovered that the four parents were almost always nuts. The kids were actually pretty normal. They were taken away from their parents due to parental neglect and abuse. Usually the teacher would see the kid wearing the same clothes every day, showing up unwashed and without having done homework. Acting out and other behavioral problems would "flag" a troubled situation. The teacher would tip off the school principal or school counselor/social worker. An investigation would ensue and the kids would be taken away and put in these places. That's how it usually worked.

My fellow inhabitants were willing to tell their stories amongst us kids. But with social workers and psychiatrists, *that* was a different matter. In those early days, my fellows would comfort me by saying that I was going to go home, that this was temporary. That was the goal we were all striving for and what we were *all* being told by the director of the place and the house parents: Our stay there was temporary and the goal for all kids was to be sent back to their parents. Yet I was *there*, at least for a time, and putting so many people together in that kind of environment is not "normal." We all had to make adjustments and everyone had their own personalities. It was quite a different experience from living at home, I can assure you of that!

For the first month and a half of my time there, my dad was still alive. He called every few days and came to visit one time on a Sunday, a few weeks after I entered the residence. He didn't look too good but it was great just to see him. We went out for a meal and chatted. It felt strange knowing I wasn't going home with him, but I told him the place was fine and I was doing fine and I looked forward to coming home. I didn't nag him or blame him (I am *very* glad for *that*). I mostly just told him what the place was like and how daily life was lived. He then dropped me off and I hugged and kissed him. I wish I had known that was the last time I would see him. A couple of weeks later, I was taking a nap on either a Saturday or Sunday afternoon. I was awakened and told my dad was on the phone. I was groggy and we spoke for a few minutes, just chitchat, nothing profound. I was more interested, frankly, in getting back to my nap. We hung up and that was the last time I spoke with him. I wish I had known that, too. The next Friday night, we were all having dinner in the big dining room/living room combo. I was tapped on the shoulder by a house parent and told to go to the director's office in the front building. I asked what for, but was told to just go. So I went. It was October 23rd at around 7:00. The director was sitting behind his desk, looking very uncomfortable and *not* looking at me. Several very uneasy seconds passed, I was simply baffled as to what was going on, and then he turned his head to stare right at me and said, "Your father's dead." I broke down uncontrollably and cried a long time. The director let me cry and then told me I was to be picked up by an aunt the next day to go to the funeral and related events. I cried all night.

The next morning, an aunt and uncle did pick me up and we went to their apartment. My family, such as it was, gathered and there were many tears. My brother Al told me what happened. He and our father had gone to dinner around 5:00 at another aunt's house. Al and Dad were sitting on the couch before dinner when our dad keeled over, hitting his head on the corner of the coffee table in front of the sofa. He turned blue. Our aunt called 911 and her husband tried to revive him, but to no avail. The ambulance came and he was DOA—dead on arrival. His fourth and final heart attack.

Our aunt and uncle had a daughter, five years my junior, and she saw my father die in front of her. My brother Allan obviously saw it as well. I have never spoken with my cousin about what she saw—she was only six at the time, and I rarely spoke with my brother about watching his father die in front of him. For Allan, it had to have been very traumatic—the swirl of emotions after all the fighting and anger between the two of them, but still the undeniable love of a son for his father and the role reversal in those last months. All this at age 18 for my oldest brother. Al was exactly, to the day, six and a half years older than I; Ron is three and a half years older than I and three years younger than Al. We each had very different relationships with our parents.

Given their early deaths, those three year differences (Al 1952, Ron 1955 and me 1959) meant worlds in terms of how we each experienced our parents. Al had many more memories of our mother, of course. He was eleven and a half when she

43

died; Ron was fifteen when our dad died. Of the three of us, though, Al had the most conflicted and complex relationships with our parents. I'm not sure he ever resolved his conflicts. He spent years in therapy, but to the limited extent he spoke with me about it, he never did settle things in his mind about either of our parents. Watching his father die under the circumstances, for Al, had to have been horrible. For anyone it would be traumatic. For Al, however, I think the trauma was intensified many times. It saddens me greatly to this day. Al died in 2007 of one massive heart attack. I miss him terribly, too.

In the days immediately after our father died, I was to stay back at our apartment in the Pomonok projects. Ron was there already (his "group residence" was much closer to our former home than my place out in Far Rockaway) and the three of us boys were reunited—for the last time—and back at the apartment in the Pomonok projects. The next week was occupied with the funeral and sitting *shiva*, the Jewish ritual of family staying together for group mourning and, as I discovered, some group healing as well. A social worker from the Far Rockaway residence came to visit one day, which I appreciated. By the end of the week, we were all telling stories and laughing, and I noticed that the ritual actually had either the intended effect or the side effect of bringing everyone together for a week to do some healing. It certainly helped.

Many people have asked why none of my relatives took my brother Ron or me into their homes, either to foster or adopt. After all, my dad had three sisters and a brother. But they were as poor as my dad. They had cramped living quarters and families of their own. I didn't believe it would be a good idea. I certainly did not ask to move in with any of them. I was uncomfortable with the idea at the time and still believe it should not have happened. I wasn't sure how discipline would have worked and how our relationship would have worked. Frankly, it was better not to be living with any of them. Uncle Meyer was not in a position to care for anyone. He was a bachelor who worked late nights and enjoyed life, if you know what I mean. He wouldn't know how to be a caregiver or father substitute if his *own life* depended upon it. Of my aunts and uncles, my favorites were Esther and Joe, but they were also living in the Pomonok projects and had one son at home and one just married. There was simply no room and no money. I didn't feel especially close to my other aunts and uncles and they weren't clamoring to take us. I got the hint that caring for us in their homes was mutually not a good idea. We briefly discussed Al becoming the guardian for Ron and me and all of us staying together, but Al was totally opposed to the idea. He was just 18 and a freshman in college, and I remembered the months earlier that year when we were left to our own devices and how badly that turned out. I knew deep down it wasn't a good idea to repeat it so it was back to Far Rockaway, but now I knew it was forever. And I did not react well to that knowledge.

I was 11 and knew I could never go back home. I was alone, way out in the far reaches of a city I hated. I had no parents and a long life stretching before me. It was a daunting set of thoughts and emotions I had to contemplate, and contemplate I did. I determined in the days after my father died that I was going to make something of myself because, after all, I had no choice.

At this point, the residence people and J.C.C.A. headquarters in Manhattan decided I needed some serious psychiatric help. So aside from social workers, there were psychologists and psychiatrists I saw. I found the whole group of them to be presumptuous, stuffy and self-important. They all had an air of superiority and haughtiness, and they seemed to pity me. They insisted that I hated my parents for "abandoning" me (their word, not mine), and I insisted they were idiots for making the suggestion. *That* did not go over well—I was being "hostile" and indeed I was! My point was that my parents died of natural causes. If they had blown their brains out in my presence telling me, "We hate you, you ruined our lives," that might be a different matter, but I simply had gotten a bad break early on, I was only 11 years old and determined to make something of myself. My persuasive powers were apparently not well developed at that early age and so there were never-ending rounds of battles with the mental health community.

To get to "the agency" headquarters in midtown Manhattan to see the social workers, psychiatrists and psychologists was quite a trek. Far Rockaway was *so far away* that the city subway system required two tokens to get on and one to get *off*. In almost all other places, one token got you on and that was it, no extra money for the privilege of *leaving*. The ride into the city was almost two hours each way. The subway was elevated for part of the way and underground for part. The above-ground route gave sweeping views of many parts of the city like Howard Beach, the Aqueduct Racetrack, Ozone Park and Kennedy Airport areas, all in Queens, and the underground part took you through some of the rougher neighborhoods in Brooklyn before getting into Manhattan. The train was the "A" train and even *then* I knew the famous song by Duke Ellington. But to go back and forth took *hours*, not including the time you actually spent talking with social workers and psychiatrists and psychologists. The vast majority of those trips I took alone, the agency wanted it that way, and we all did it at our appointed times. Back then, it simply was not unusual to let kids roam frequently all over the city.

These days, it's scandalous, which shows you how times have changed.

Those long trips gave me lots of time to think. I would sometimes read books or newspapers to help pass the time, but often I would just look out the window or think about things. I enjoyed the time alone to think. I thought about all sorts of things, but mostly politics, philosophy and life. I thought about what I would do with my life, what I *could* do with my life, and I dreamed of the day when I would be grown up and free.

The social workers and psychiatrists I saw were mostly wasted time. They seemed to think I was going to simply trust them immediately and pour out my heart to them. I told them they needed to earn my trust, something they never tried to do, as if the simple role they occupied obviated the need for them to relate to me as a human being. I kept telling them that I did not want to see them, did not want to talk with them and often, we would literally just sit there staring at each other for an hour or so with total silence in the room. It was *very* weird, but I enjoyed getting out to travel into and roam Manhattan and find good things to eat along the way. So to me, the time spent at the agency was the price I paid for getting the day off from school to go into "the city."

The bathroom at the Far Rockaway residence had a nice tub in the back that no one ever seemed to use. So I made it my own and some nights I would soak in the tub before bed. It would be quiet and I would think about my circumstances, what would come next for me and give myself pep talks to keep going forward. I reminded myself I was still just a kid and my whole life lay ahead of me. I was comforting myself, and it worked. I was learning perspective without even knowing it! When I told these things to the social workers and psychiatrists, they didn't seem to believe me—and frankly, I really didn't care what they thought and told them as much. They didn't react well to *that*, and I took some delight in the fact that I frustrated them. They seemed to think they could "fix" me and I didn't want whatever they were peddling for a "fix." I was happy to content myself with the thought that I was not "broken" and would figure things out for myself.

The sixth grade passed uneventfully enough. I made friends with most of the other kids in the residence and school was school. It was just another public school. The other kids in the residence were mostly pretty normal; the home itself was in the community; we could go to the movies (and did) and play in the yard (basketball and stickball were popular); and were reasonably free to roam around the area. There was the YMHA next door. We would spend a good deal of time there listening to music, playing various sports, and just hanging around. I found my first girlfriend there. She was a nice, cute kid who lived in the neighborhood. We didn't do anything serious, just fooled around the way pre-teens and young teens did in those days.

Once sixth grade ended and then summer, it was on to "junior high school"—the fall of 1971. That is when things went really badly. The sixth grade was in a decent neighborhood with a decent walk to school and back. Seventh grade involved a bus ride into a very rough neighborhood. It was back to being mugged and I was not happy. Also, I contracted lice, and that is a bad thing to happen to anyone. One day as I was in the bathroom at the stand-up urinal, I felt a cold pointed thing on my neck and a young African American male was saying he wanted my money. I asked him if I could finish peeing and he stepped back. I then gave him my money and decided that I didn't want to be in that school any longer. Of course, reading a book in class and seeing bugs fall from your head onto the book is not fun either. The shampoos and all did not work and I finally got a basic buzz cut to rid myself of the little beasties. I told the folks at the residence that I would like a transfer to another of their facilities and they turned down my request.

The school did not get any better, my studies fell off dramatically and I decided that drastic action was needed. So I did my best acting job, moped around for a few days and then walked into the director's office, telling him I was going to kill myself because I was very unhappy and my prospects were bleak. They wouldn't let me out of that place and I had seen the whole crime-and-bugs-movie already and didn't like it one bit. The director didn't seem to take me seriously except the next day they drove me to Elmhurst General Hospital in another part of Queens, and locked me in a teenage psychiatric unit. Hell, mission accomplished! I was out of the residence! Twelve years old and in a locked psychiatric ward. It was on the next-to-top floor of a very large building, the windows were all sealed with locked grates over them and the ward was locked in the front. The ward itself was large, with a huge communal bathroom. If you read the book or saw the movie *One Flew Over The Cuckoo's Nest*, it was something akin to that. It was a good-sized ward with three kids to a room, about 18 kids total, and they had a pool table in the ward. I got very good at playing pool. I'd never played before, but practice makes perfect and I had a good deal of time to practice.

At one end of the ward, there was a large window (sealed and grated, but you could still see out) and that window looked out over a part of Queens. In the foreground, the elevated Number 7 subway train ran by as it went through Elmhurst. This was a few miles from Flushing and in-between Flushing and Manhattan, not far from Shea Stadium where the Mets played baseball. I knew the area pretty well. I often watched the trains go by and longed for restoration of my freedom. (Ironically, six years later, when I first moved out on my own after graduating high school, I had an apartment not very far from that hospital, and would walk near it often. It never failed to remind me of things past and always put me in a reflective mood.)

They subjected me to *lots* of drugs while there. I was incarcerated on December 10, 1971 and forced to drink liquid Mellaril and take pill forms of Thorazine, Elavil and Stelazine. These are very powerful drugs used to treat schizophrenia, depression and heaven knows what else, and the liquid Mellaril tasted like horse manure. Needless to say, I was pretty sleepy most of the time. (About a year after discharge from the hospital, when I first tried marijuana, nothing happened. I tried it again and felt a little sensation. I described the feeling of light headedness, altered perception, giddiness and dry mouth to the kids I was smoking with, and they told me I was "stoned." I said "you must be kidding. You should have had the stuff they gave me in the hospital. Now *that* shit was kickass—this is like cotton candy." It was true then and remains true to this day. The legal stuff has it over reefer hands down.)

The remnants of my family came to visit and they were very concerned—hell, so was I—but 33 days inside was a fascinating experience. During that time I had taken up smoking cigarettes and unlike current times, *anyone* could get smokes in those days. I was allowed to smoke in the hospital, when I was awake, that is.

I made a couple of friends there in Elmhurst General. One was a big red-headed Irish kid who was 15 and committed because he got drunk in a bar and got into one hellacious fight (he said he hit a cop over the head with a chair and I didn't doubt him). Another was a kid about my size who threatened to kill his parents. That *will* get you incarcerated! One of the kids in that locked ward was very rebellious and would regularly throw major fits—loud and violent. On those occasions, the attendants (all large men) would hold him down and the nurse would administer an injection with a big needle of some powerful liquid that would knock him out for hours. Like I said, an interesting experience. And, more psychiatrists. The one assigned to me was an older lady with a thick German accent and a really butch haircut. I thought I was going to Auschwitz for sure!

A big record hit at that time was Sly & The Family Stone's "Family Affair," and it got played endlessly on the record player in the ward. To this day, I cannot hear that song without immediately going back in time to that hospital ward. I have my crew play "Family Affair" as filler music on our radio show from time to time, just to remind me of what a long, strange trip it's been—my apologies to the Grateful Dead!

I was at Elmhurst General Hospital over Christmas and New Year's and discharged on January 13, 1972 (yes, I remember all this, including the dates) and sent back to Far Rockaway. Of course, they sent me back to the same junior high school and I repeated my requests for transfer. I got my wish. In April 1972, after about 18 months in Far Rockaway and Elmhurst General Hospital, I was shipped to the Pleasantville Cottage School in Pleasantville, New York, about 35 miles north of New York City in Westchester County.

• • •

In April 2004, I was on a trip with my wife and in-laws back to New York. Early on a Saturday morning, I woke up and, with Frances still sleeping, took that Number 7 subway out to the last stop in Queens, which is downtown Flushing, and got a cab to LaGuardia Airport to pick up a rental car. Since I knew New York well and Frances and my in-laws did not, the plan was for me to get that rental car that early Saturday morning. I knew when we mapped the trip out a couple of months earlier, what that morning would be like. I had an odd feeling as I retraced old steps throughout the New York City subway system. Once on the Number 7 train going through Queens, I got out on the platform by Elmhurst General and just stood there, leaning against the railing, staring into *that very window I had stared out of more than 30 years earlier,* and cried my eyes out. Fortunately no one else was there—it was very early on Saturday morning—but it sure helped give me perspective.

I got on the next train and once I got the rental car, took a tour of all my old stomping grounds in Flushing and nearby parts of Queens. I cried the whole time. I saw my elementary school and reflected back on that morning when my dad first dropped me off for the third grade and I felt so alone and cried on the schoolyard. I went past our old apartment in Pomonok. I went to the place where my dad died (right across from Queens College) and places in Queens that played a role throughout my early life. I was looking at all the places where significant and sad parts of my life happened. It was a very emotional day.

* * * * *

4

THEY DON'T CALL IT PLEASANTVILLE FOR NOTHING

Named after the town nearby where Pace College and Reader's Digest were headquartered, one of the key benefits of the Pleasantville Cottage School was permission to smoke. In those days, even though the law said you had to be 18 to smoke, no one obeyed the law; anyone could buy and smoke cigarettes. In Far Rockaway, they definitely did not want me smoking. In Elmhurst General and Pleasantville, no problem. Art Buchwald (long-time newspaper writer, humorist, satirist and screen writer) came from a broken home and spent time at Pleasantville. He went there to film a fundraising video for the place while I was there. I didn't meet him although I read his work even then.

There were approximately 160 kids there. Each cottage (and yes, they even looked like cottages) had 16 kids. The place looked like one of the summer camps I attended as a kid, just with a school on the grounds. It was situated on about 150 very pretty, well-kept wooded acres with a big administration building where the social workers, psychiatrists and "supervisors" worked. A group of house parents worked in each cottage. The school was staffed by teachers with special education degrees, and the classes ranged from elementary grades to high school. The school building was large, modern and well furnished. Near the school were a large gymnasium and a good-sized baseball field. Like I said, summer camp with a school but you lived there year-round, and trips off the grounds were only allowed with permission. That many of us took the liberty of sneaking off grounds was a given. Sometimes caught and stripped of privileges, sometimes not, it was a game of cat and mouse. There were no fences around the place. The easiest way to get out was to walk through the woods behind the school building. There was a road that led into Thornwood, a small town adjacent to Pleasantville Cottage School. The town of Pleasantville itself was further away. A very long walk, it was better to get a ride into Pleasantville, which was a typical suburban town and a lot larger than Thornwood. However, for sneaking-off purposes, Thornwood was adequate—a short enough walk and a couple of stores.

The cottages were grouped by age and gender and there were more boys than girls. I was in Cottage 9. All the cottages looked the same; each was a self-contained house with a living room, kitchen, dining room and upstairs. There was a very large communal bathroom centrally located and accessible to all the bedrooms. There were two, three or four boys to a room and the kids were still mostly normal, but a few seemed to be in serious need of help.

In all three of the residences I was in, I got to know a lot of my fellow cohabitants well and, for the most part, the vast majority had no business being in those places. My story was *very* unusual—an orphan with no place to go. Easily 90% or more of the kids had the "four live parents thing" that I described earlier. As I would observe these parents on visitors day, I was relieved to be an orphan with the parents I had been born with. The parents of the other kids were nuts and they often had young children with them. I dubbed these young kids "the next generation of inmates" and I genuinely felt lucky that my parents were normal, they just died of organic diseases but left me without too much baggage and a full life ahead of me to make of it as I could. My fellow inmates had live, ongoing, new situations to deal with, new troubles all the time, and a dynamic situation with four crazy parents awaiting them every day.

While I did not often get visitors, I did get weekends occasionally to go back to "the city" and be with my aunts and brothers. I would go into the city by train (the agency paid for the trip) and spend a couple of days with one or the other of my aunts and uncles, and go see my brothers. Since I knew my way around the city, I traveled alone by subway and bus.

Between the ages of 13 and 14 and while living in Pleasantville (it was actually a very nice bedroom community of New York City; a pleasant commuter train ride into Manhattan), I was given a little job after school—to tutor the youngest kids, who were in a cottage not far from me. They were eight and nine year-old boys. As I helped them with their homework, I got to know them. They were nice, sweet little kids, as normal as any their age, and I started asking them questions like, "How'd a nice kid like you get into a place like this?" They told me stories of abuse, neglect and abandonment that made my blood boil. I'll spare you the stories, but suffice it to say I formed the opinion that parents need to be licensed, and that the *parents* of the kids in these institutions needed to be institutionalized while the kids should be set free. I continue to hold these beliefs, as all the evidence I have seen since reinforces my earlier opinions. The *adults* are crazy, the kids innocent victims.

As with the residence in Far Rockaway, I got to know my fellow inmates (or whatever you want to call them) and grew stronger in my belief that I was the lucky one. When I was in Far Rockaway, I had done well on the aptitude tests and was put in the "AP" or "Advanced Placement" classes in the junior high school. That ended with all the trouble I had there, but when I got to Pleasantville, they tested me again and skipped me from seventh grade to ninth grade. I'll be the first to admit I was a big intellectual fish swimming in a small intellectual pond but compared to my fellows, I was pretty bright. Teachers and house parents took an extra interest in me, encouraging me to make something of myself. I had long chats with several of the house parents and teachers over the years I was in all these places, and they were mostly very sympathetic to my plight. They encouraged me to get an education and push the limits of my natural gifts.

The teachers would come into the cottages some days after school to help tutor us with our homework. One day in the cottage, I was being a smart ass with one of my teachers—a small but muscular ex-drill sergeant-type who was totally bald, had piercing blue eyes and smoked Camel non-filters regularly. He was about 65 and looked 55. He paced relentlessly and was a coarse bundle of energy. He was *not* the guy to be a smart ass with, but I did it anyway. He grabbed me by my shirt collar, literally threw me against a wall and got nose-to-nose with me. He said in a semi-loud but stern voice, "Listen kid, you got a chance. You have a brain. Look around you. The best these other kids can hope for is to be a New York City garbage man. You can make something of yourself—don't fuck it up!" That had a lasting impression on me, as you can probably tell.

I was a mess in those days. Very rebellious, not particularly focused on education, but reading things on my own like *One*

Flew Over The Cuckoo's Nest and *Catcher In The Rye*. One house parent gave me *Siddhartha* and he was ridiculed by another house parent, but I read that too. I was deemed one of the brighter, better adjusted kids in the Pleasantville Cottage School, and at the start of tenth grade, was part of an experiment. I, and a handful of other kids deemed worthy, were sent to Briarcliff High School, an outside public school. It was located in Briarcliff Manor, the next town over from Pleasantville. In those days, Briarcliff Manor was one of the wealthiest suburbs in one of the wealthiest counties (Westchester County) in the United States. What was reputedly the Rockefeller estate was literally on the way from the Pleasantville Cottage School to Briarcliff High School. We saw glimpses of it through the trees and shrubs and chain link fence while we rode to school on the small school bus that ferried us to and from school each day. It looked like one of those medieval baronies depicted in the history books—endless grounds of rolling hills with immaculately manicured lawns.

The kids at Briarcliff High came from well-off families, living in very nice houses. The school grounds were well-kept and expansive. There was a tennis court—something new to me! The school curriculum was very advanced and demanding. The teachers were equally demanding. For me, it was a shock. I wasn't ready and flunked out in a short time. I simply could not keep up with the pace of the lessons and the shock of the environment. The Briarcliff kids didn't take well to us either. Mostly, the group of us stayed to ourselves.

I was sent back to the school on the grounds at Pleasantville and was both relieved and angry at myself for the failed experiment. Over time, most of the other kids flunked out too, though one or two continued on. It was just a rough time for all of us.

Chances are you know something of recent American history so when I tell you I was in the Pleasantville Cottage School from 1972-1974, you should think Richard Nixon. And when you think Richard Nixon, you should think Watergate. I was still a political junkie; that had not changed. I had continued my reading and was glued to the television set with the Watergate hearings. I talked politics with the house parents and teachers and found the whole process fascinating—I still do.

By the time I turned 13, I was in Pleasantville Cottage School, the middle of the three places I was in for those six years between 11 and 17. Mostly to please my father's sisters but also because I knew, as is the tradition, I would receive gifts of money, I got myself Bar Mitzvah. The training for this actually began in Far Rockaway shortly before I was hospitalized at Elmhurst General. The rabbi bore an uncanny resemblance to my dad in facial appearance, size and body structure. This creeped me out, as you can imagine. I didn't share this with anyone at the time and gamely soldiered on, figuring it was simply a coincidence and not God torturing me. Once ensconced in Pleasantville, a new rabbi took over my Bar Mitzvah training and, on the appointed day, my aunts and uncles all trooped up into Westchester County and watched me perform the rites of passage. They seemed proud and I was glad I made them happy, as I knew it would have made my dad happy. I also enjoyed the cash bestowed on me. As with most kids of that age, regardless of the religion, once the ceremony was over, I was done with religion, certainly organized religion.

Back in the Cottage for the party after the Bar Mitzvah, I got the first inkling of my future as "NorMan GoldMan." There was a big cake with "Congratulations Norman Goldman" written on it. One of the house parents suggested I get two pieces of cake—each cut with only the word "man" in it since the Bar Mitzvah ceremony signifies the growth from boy to man. (There is no "teenager" in Jewish culture, or most cultures, for that matter.) And so it was—I got my two pieces of cake, and each said "man."

Life in each of these places was different—different from "normal" life and different from each of the other institutions within the agency. The kids, myself included, adapted and learned to adapt because we had no choice *but* to adapt. There were occasional fights and the entire range of things that kids do, we did. Kids broke into other kids' lockers and stole stuff, just like school generally, and taunted and played touch football and baseball and all the rest. But what strikes me now is how little sexual trouble we had. There were no instances of rape, pregnancy or "experimentation" other than the usual teen necking back behind the stands or in dark corners, same as happens everywhere. There were no instances of house parents raping or inappropriately touching kids. (Some years ago, around 2000, I read of an instance in Pleasantville where some girls threw acid in the face of a house parent. I was long gone by then.) Given all that is happening in society *these* days, *those* days (the early and mid-1970s) seem very innocent.

After three and a half years of being with J.C.C.A. (18 months in Far Rockaway and the Elmhurst General Hospital experience) and two years in Pleasantville, I was 15 and transferred to a "group residence" back in Queens, New York City. My failed experiment at Briarcliff High School behind me, I was to finish tenth grade at Newtown High School, a short walk from Elmhurst General Hospital.

* * * * *

5

BACK TO THE CITY

It was April 1974 and I was being driven by one of the house parents of Cottage 9 back to Queens. I packed up my few belongings, put them into the car (the agency had cars and many house parents had cars they would use to ferry us around) and away we went. I was happy to be leaving Pleasantville knowing I was going to my last group residence, and was one step closer to freedom. The group residence (we simply called it "the residence") was in an area of Queens called Rego Park. It was not far from the better-known Forest Hills (where the famous tennis tournament is held) and also not far from Jackson Heights where Don Rickles and Carroll O'Connor (Archie Bunker) grew up. These two gents are the most famous graduates of Newtown High School.

My brother Ron spent three years in a residence just like the one I was about to join. His was a block away from the one I was moving into. Ron was 15 when our dad died. He was just starting the tenth grade and spent his last three years of high school at Newtown. "Newtown" was a misnomer since the building dated from the late 1800s, and looked it.

It was the typical condition of many New York City public schools. Compare *that* with Briarcliff High School and you get a good glimpse of the two Americas John Edwards talked about when he was running for President. At that time, in the early and mid-1970s when Ron and I were in the Rego Park residences, there were five group residences run by the J.C.C.A. within a three block area—three for boys and two for girls. Each was identical in layout. The agency had rented two, three bedroom apartments at the end of hallways in regular apartment buildings. These were the largest apartments in the buildings. What separated the two apartments was one wall— the apartments were mirror images of each other. As part of the deal with the private landlord that owned these regular apartment buildings, they busted out the wall that separated the apartments to create one large, ten room, six bedroom group residence. Each residence had two living rooms, two bathrooms, two kitchens and six bedrooms.

By the time I got to the one in Rego Park, the last of the three for me, Ron had already graduated high school and moved out on his own. He took an apartment elsewhere in Queens and began college at Queens College, across from the apartment where our dad had died, right there at the Pomonok housing projects. Al was also attending Queens College and their time there overlapped by a year.

The residences were next to the Long Island Expressway. Ron had been in the first apartment building on one side of the highway while mine was one block further away. The group of apartment buildings covered several square blocks and were identical, save for their addresses. The other tenants in these buildings knew who we were and what these residences were all about and had various reactions. Some of our neighbors were friendly, others not so much. There were house parents in each of these places. They had one bedroom and each of the kids were two to a room. One house parent stayed in the apartment at any given time. They would each work three and a half days continuously. As with house parents in the other places, these were mostly graduate students who had inexpensive apartments on the outside where they would live when they were not staying at the residence. While the agency did not pay them a lot of money, food and part-time lodging were part of the deal and that is never a bad thing if you are a graduate student on a budget. During Ron's stay and at the very beginning of my time in the residences at Rego Park, young married couples were the house parents—these were always the best situations, as the young marrieds were cool and pretty relaxed about the rules.

Since these apartments were in normal apartment buildings in regular urban neighborhoods, we were back in the city. They were a far cry from the summer camp-like atmosphere and physical setting of Pleasantville and a far cry from Far Rockaway which, while still a house in a neighborhood, was way out in the boondocks. I was happy to be back in Queens with closer access to both my brothers. I knew my way around easily and the subway was just a couple of short blocks away. (I did not mention this earlier, but shortly after my mother died, I broke my right arm badly by tripping and falling into a wall at our apartment in Brooklyn. My dad was shocked and overwhelmed, as was I; it looked terrible. They set it and cast it at a hospital in Brooklyn. My arm was in a cast for weeks but the doctor who did my aftercare had an office in a new set of very nice apartment buildings called Lefrak City, just off the Long Island Expressway in Queens. I remember my dad taking me there for checkups and to have the cast removed and I wanted to live *there*—it was so nice. These group residences were right next to Lefrak City. I was back on familiar ground!)

Since the residence was for kids in high school, the rules were somewhat looser. Curfews were later (we were getting older) and some of the kids had part-time jobs after school for pocket money. These jobs were typical teenage jobs. Bagging groceries was popular and since there were lots of stores around, jobs were not difficult to find. I registered at Newtown High School, adjusted quickly and easily (I was getting to be a pro at this orphanage thing) and didn't have the kinds of academic troubles I had at Briarcliff High School. The two years I spent at this last group residence passed quickly, and I was able to get a hands-on introduction to two of my passions: politics and radio!

I was 15 and just finishing my sophomore year in high school. I had decent enough grades in school (Briarcliff High notwithstanding). By the time I finished my sophomore year, I was generally a "B" student, but I was restless. I discovered at the very end of the school year that there was an "internship program" (I had to find out what *that* was) that would allow me to work *outside* of school, not attend *any* classes, but get full credit for a whole semesters' worth of classes. This was the program for me! The students would work full-time four days a week at a location under supervision. Then on Friday, there was a workshop at a school administration building in Manhattan where we would discuss our experiences. Each week, one kid did a kind of show-and-tell about his internship. I got in touch with the guidance counselor and found there was an opening in Queens Borough Hall to work with the Assistant Borough President for Senior Citizen and Consumer Affairs. I was on my way!

I started the fall semester in September 1974, not in classrooms, but in Queens Borough Hall. I loved that work.

The young man who was the Assistant Borough President was as delightful and decent a human being as you will ever find. He was a perfect mentor with a heart as big as all outdoors. He loved doing good works for people and was a terrific teacher.

The work was fascinating—Richard Nixon had just signed the SSI Program into law and we were helping to get outreach going to the aged, blind and disabled people who would benefit from the program. The "kneeling buses" (they actually come down, so that people with problems taking big steps up could get on buses) were being put on the street—more outreach needed. It was now the fall of 1974 and I was starting to feel like I could see a light at the end of the orphanage tunnel.

Because Queens Borough Hall was a unit of New York City government, it was impossible to keep politics out of the place. And since I had loved politics from the time I was a tiny tot, I said I'd like to get involved in actual politics, and my supervisor there arranged for me to work on the Hugh Carey for Governor Campaign. I worked, not only by day in the office, but then at night and on weekends went to the local campaign office where I made phone calls (phone banking) and walked the neighborhoods giving out leaflets and doing whatever odd jobs (stuffing and licking envelopes) I could do to help. I even got to meet the candidate one evening shortly before the election. I was thrilled! I was 15 and loving politics. I was fascinated by the machinery of the whole thing and how easy it was for citizens to get involved! One of Hugh Carey's big issues was to close down the horrors that were the state mental hospitals. They had become torture chambers of neglect and abuse. The local news had done an expose on Willowbrook Hospital and then-Congressman Carey grabbed hold of the issue and made it a big deal in the campaign. Democrats care! I figured that one out for myself long before I was 15.

The then-Queens Borough President was named Donald Manes (pronounced man-ess). He was a machine politician if ever there was one. I got to meet him during that internship and it was exciting. A real celebrity! Unfortunately some years later, Donald Manes, was caught fixing parking tickets and involved in other corruption. He committed suicide, but only after a couple of failed attempts. He did it ultimately in his living room in front of his family. It must have been a devastating experience for them. Like I said, I was the lucky one—my parents didn't kill themselves and die in shame and scandal.

I also got some jobs while in this residence, doing odds and ends, and I discovered I *really* enjoyed smoking pot! There was a hill on the side of the Long Island Expressway, a sloping, grassy hill just a block from the residence, where kids from all over the neighborhood would congregate, especially on Friday and Saturday nights. Ron had told me about this hill; what he experienced continued during my time. The hill was large and had an imaginary line down the center—the "juicers" took one side and the "smokers" took the other. You could easily tell who was who. The juicers were loud, drunk, fighting and cursing; the smokers were mellow and quiet. I was proud to be a smoker! We had a lot of fun on that hill; the guys in my residence were a reasonably cohesive bunch. We all got along and we often stayed together and walked to school together and so forth.

They *still* made me see social workers. There were *more* trips into the agency headquarters in Manhattan; albeit and mercifully, shorter subway trips, but one of the social workers (indeed, the last one) was the worst of the bunch. A young, preppy, upper middle class snob, this woman (*not* Miss Lewinsky) set new records for haughtiness and snootiness.

I just don't react well to that kind of person. Of the social workers I had been compelled to see, most were women, a couple were men and I was unimpressed with the lot. Some were worse than others and this last one refused to leave me alone. All I asked was to simply *not* be forced to see her. She and the rest of the agency people (there were supervisors on top of supervisors) insisted I keep the appointments they kept setting, but she did not like me sitting there quiet, letting the time pass until I could go like many of the other social workers had been content to do. So I started reading Freud and Jung and other books on psychology and talking psychology with her. *That* did not go over well, so I did even more of it. One of my favorites was *The Fifty Minute Hour* by Dr. Robert Lindner about the most unusual cases he had as a psychiatrist. I confess I was being an asshole and, yes, I had a lot of hostility in me. But I had requested, nicely, to be left alone; just let me finish out my sentence and go away upon high school graduation, but they refused, so I fought back. After awhile, this social worker wearied of the aggravation I was causing and finally relented and left me alone. Mission accomplished! And years ahead of George W. Bush!

There were some odd characters in all these orphanages, none odder than a kid that I'll call "Derek" (not his real name). I met Derek in this last group residence. We were the same age. Derek was essentially abandoned by his alcoholic father when he was about five; his mother had already vanished. He still stayed in his father's apartment, but he was like Tarzan—raised on the streets by whomever he could find. All this in the South Bronx, one of the roughest neighborhoods in the city. Derek missed most, if not all, of the socializing skills that any child should be given. Derek, though, had grown up with some sense of things. He was just a very odd duck. He was also a handsome kid and a young lady magnet! Of course, he cycled through girlfriends quickly. Once they got to know him, they were gone. He enjoyed shocking people and for some reason he *really* liked me. Oh joy! Derek would do things like walk up to me and say, "Hey Norm, smell my fingers" and I would say, "Derek, I don't want to smell your fingers" and he would say, "But I just fingered this girl and you gotta smell this." I respectfully declined. Like I said, he was odd. Another time, I was walking to my room and Derek was in the hallway outside the bathroom. He said, "Hey Norm, come here." He motioned inside the bathroom. He pointed. In the toilet was a huge dump. I looked at him with true disgust on my face, and he said, with an impish smile, "I went logging." One last Derek story. Late one afternoon, I was in my room doing my homework. Derek's room was next to mine. Piercing the silence came a holler like, well, Tarzan. I jumped over to Derek's room and there he was, totally naked, standing in the window frame (two tall, narrow casement windows, with cranks on either side to open and close them, and a strip of metal in the middle) hanging out the window, holding onto that middle metal strip with his left hand while exposed for all the world to see and doing his best Tarzan yells. I could see people on the street looking up at our third-story apartment. The house parent on duty also heard the commotion, and came running. An older woman, rather prim and proper, she took one look and nearly fainted. I told Derek to get out of the window, which he did. Not long after, Derek was booted out of the place; heaven only knows whatever happened to him. By this time, I was 16 years old and had quite a life already!

There were other troubled kids in all these places, but not as many as you'd think. Most of the kids were reasonably normal, certainly no less troubled than other kids outside these places. But there were some odd ones and some of them had difficulty handling the bad situations imposed on them. Many of them became my friends and I felt genuinely sorry for them. They got bad breaks as kids, just like me, but didn't do well handling them. Of course, I wasn't sure how *I* was doing either at that point, but I always had enough confidence that I could eventually right the ship, get myself squared away and lead a good life. For these troubled kids, I felt badly that they had lives stretching before them with perhaps not the best outcomes ahead.

Since I skipped a year of school upon my arrival at Pleasantville, I was a grade ahead of where I should have been. I was slated to graduate high school at 17. Around this time, I was at a party at one of the girls' group residences that the agency maintained in the neighborhood. It was either a Friday or Saturday night. There was this pretty blond standing there all by herself so I decided to go introduce myself. We chatted amicably for a few minutes and then her boyfriend came over. Whoops! My bad. I decided to simply stay and talk with them both. While the young lady was still in high school, her boyfriend had just started college at New York University (NYU) in Greenwich Village, lower Manhattan. It came up in the three-way conversation that he worked at the NYU radio station. I told him I'd always loved radio and he said, "Why don't you come on down? We can always use help." He explained that, as a college radio station, there was no pay in the deal and that everyone there was doing it for credit or interest in a possible future radio career. He told me where it was so I decided to go down there as soon as I could. And I did. I showed up and introduced myself around and simply started working. I began news writing and they explained that, in order to touch the knobs and buttons on the control board,

I would need a 3rd Class FCC license; it's just like a learner's permit, but a bit more challenging.

I went down to the Federal Building (close to the Twin Towers that came down on September 11, 2001) and got the booklet. I studied and passed the test! I started working at the station one day a week—on Friday afternoons and evenings. The station (WNYU 89.1 FM—it's still on the air to this day) did a 30-minute newscast called *The Evening Report* at 7 p.m. I loved it and got to know some of the college kids who worked there. They started liking me; I started liking them. I was dependable, I showed up when I said I would and worked hard, and began to imagine a career in radio.

I simply *loved* being at that radio station and learning *everything* I could possibly learn! But there was one problem: The agency and that social worker I talked about earlier (and her supervisor, another social worker I did not care for) were *dead set against it*. They argued that I should spend more time with my housemates. I needed their permission, since I was a ward of the state, and would be away for dinner on Friday evenings and wouldn't get back until late since I was socializing with my new friends after the show was over at 7:30. I said I was going to do it no matter what they said; all they could do was expel me, unless they were interested in chaining me to a fence somewhere. One house parent took up my cause and, in time, the social workers relented—the squeaky wheel *really does* get the grease—and I was free to pursue my radio career! I spent five years working there part-time, and got to know lots of students, some of whom are on radio and television today. I spent countless hours there and loved it all.

I cannot leave the topic of my years in the orphanages (group residences, institutions, whatever) without some final notes. One time in Far Rockaway and one time in Pleasantville,

I ran away. The time I ran from the residence at Far Rockaway, it was after the hospitalization and shortly before the transfer to Pleasantville. Heck, that might have been the last straw. They figured, get me out to a more isolated place! I took the subway to my brother Al's apartment in Jamaica, Queens. Al wasn't home, so I was hanging around in front of his building waiting for him when I hooked up with some teenagers and young adults who invited me to go drinking with them. I was just turning 13, and we had a great time—stayed out most of the night drinking, playing pool and telling jokes. I got lucky; they were regular guys who thought it was fun to carouse with a kid and nothing bad happened except I got drunk, but it was fun. When I knocked on Al's door at about 4 a.m. he was pretty upset! I told him I wanted to come live with him but he refused. He called the residence and they sent a houseparent in a car to come get me.

When I ran away from Pleasantville, it was with another kid and we took the train into the city and went to his mom's apartment in the Bronx. His mom was one of the crazy parents. She told us to go back, and wasn't nice about how she said it. I called my brother Al (again) and he (again) refused to let me come live with him. The Pleasantville people eventually figured out where we were since two of us were gone, called my friend's mom, she turned us in and another car came to pick us up and bring us back.

As you can probably guess, I was very unhappy in these places. The days passed like weeks. I chafed under their authority. I was rebellious and became a leader among my fellows, fomenting trouble, like strikes (no chores if no extra privileges) or leaving the grounds for unauthorized little trips to Thornwood. Now that I am older, six years time passage seems like nothing. Six years passes in the blink of an eye.

But when you're 11 years old, six years seems like an eternity. And it did seem like an eternity. I was rambunctious and kept demanding to be let out. I wanted to get my own apartment, get a job and be on my own. I resented their authority over me and really resented their constant procession of social workers, psychiatrists and psychologists, who I got into the habit of taunting and mocking. I was a handful and couldn't wait to get out, dreaming of the day I would be free.

I saw my brothers fairly regularly during the six years I spent in the orphanages. Depending upon where I was at the time, I would see them more or less—in Far Rockaway, not too often; in Pleasantville, with its generally once-per-month "city trips" home, I would see them then; in the last place, the group residence in Rego Park, I saw them more often. We would go to ballgames (the Mets, in particular) or just hang around in Al's apartment listening to music and talking. One day when I was about 14, before getting on the Number 7 train to Shea Stadium (during a Pleasantville "city trip"), I persuaded Al to buy me a tall can of beer. I drank it on the train and got a nice buzz on before the ballgame. For some things, New York was wonderful; no one on that train batted an eyelash at a young teenager swigging a can of beer. But for the most part, reefer was my drug of choice—alcohol never really did much for me.

A lot of the time in these places we did things all kids do. We played baseball, touch football, basketball. We did our homework, we watched television and we hung around telling stories and talking about our lives. We made friends with some, were just civil with others. We did our best to cope with the situations in which we found ourselves. I was generally one of the leaders. I was looked to for brains (we were *all* in trouble!) because I liked to read and was interested in current events; I watched the news and was fascinated with politics. Most of the other kids were not bookworms and they generally looked to me to be a leader among them. I was friendly with most kids in all of these places. Despite there being cliques, everyone generally agreed that "Norm was all right." I thought of myself as "the bridge"; I was able to get along with the various cliques and kids and was able to communicate with everyone, even if when they didn't get along with each other. I spent much of those years simply trying to gain my footing. For a lot of the time I was a mess—physically sloppy, a restive, restless, antsy mess. I needed to do a lot of work on myself and was doing my best with what guidance I could get and what self-discovery I could muster.

I spent countless hours thinking about politics, reading the newspapers and books and listening to the news. Though I had debates and discussions, I came by my views by methodically working through issues and principles, usually by myself. I debated with myself, taking different sides and thinking about things alone. In a very real way, I was self-taught. I still do a lot of this type of reasoning now.

The summer of 1976 was my last summer in the group residence. Shortly after I graduated high school, I got a job in Coney Island as a shipping clerk. It was a physically hard job, carrying heavy boxes around. I realized that physical labor was not for me so I hustled to get into college. The foreman there was a huge, strapping Hungarian immigrant with a thick accent and not much of an intellectual. I told him I was going to college and he said, "Ah, brain work. Bad. You get headaches! I work hard all day, go home, take shower, and feel great. You should do what I do." I decided against that course of action!

I knew that I could get Social Security and Veterans benefits, as my brothers before me had done, so I took my S.A.T. scores (very high in English, very low in math) and applied to the free college in New York City, City University of New York. I had a solid "B" average for high school and figured I could get into Queens College where both my brothers had gone. But I was wrong. My grades were not good enough so I got my second choice, Hunter College. This turned out well since Hunter was right in the middle of Manhattan—the heart of the action—even though I had to spend a lot more time on those damn subways! I spent that last summer working and planning to leave the "agency." In reality, in the deep back part of my mind, I wanted to leave New York and go to college in Florida. I'd never been there, but I knew the weather was great and I wanted out of New York! I just didn't have the guts or the fortitude to go through all I needed to do to go down that road, like scholarships and such; it took all my courage to arrange for college in New York. But my long term goal was to move away to some place warm.

It should be apparent by now that without substantial government investment in me, I would not or could not be in a position to succeed. The Jewish Child Care Association took substantial government money. The need was (and still is) large; too large for private charity and its dependence on the whims of the donors. The Social Security benefits that my brothers and I received enabled us to go to college. The free public university in New York City gave us a great chance at higher education. The Jewish Family Service (a private charity) and the free summer camps (also a private charity) augmented the public resources, but could never replace them. I was given encouragement by the house parents, teachers and many others along the way. I was given the resources to put me in a position to succeed. I understand that now and I understood it then. This is why I am, in part, who I am.

· · · · ·

6

FINALLY ON MY OWN

On September 1, 1976, I was free to leave. I needed to move somewhere, so my brother Ron arranged to have me share a space with one of his friends who was looking for an apartment. We found a place just eight or so blocks from my last group residence. This young man was a few years older and had been in the residence with Ron. We rented a "garden apartment" close to Newtown High School and I arranged to get my Social Security and Veterans Administration benefits. September 3rd came and no check from Social Security. A crisis, as soon as I was free! I quickly ran out of money. My roommate was terrific in helping me survive, but I fell into a steep depression. I didn't attend school much and was barely eating. It was a horrible three months and a terrible way to start my long anticipated freedom. I was applying for welfare benefits (literally, I had the application in hand) when, on December 9th, the Social Security checks arrived and included all the missed months. I got caught up with the money I owed everyone (I had borrowed what I could; it was a demoralizing experience) and established a routine. I got going in college and got acclimated to being my own disciplinarian. It was a bumpy start—having to shop for myself and do the laundry and the household chores and not having much money, limited my options. All the romanticism I had envisioned of being on my own was simply not there. And being in New York, being poor *really* made you feel poor!

After those first few horrible months, I managed to right the ship and got into a routine. College was great. I found professors and courses I loved (of course, politics, sociology and history) and found part-time work doing public opinion polls for the Harris Poll (Lou Harris) and some local pollsters. The work was fascinating—I got to talk politics for money! I did surveys on the telephone all over the United States; usually they were political polls. The pay was better than minimum wage, the hours flexible and during breaks in school, I could work full time. Most of the people working there (students and out-of-work actors) hated the work and lasted a month or less. I lasted two years! The only reason I left was because I got a dream political job working for Congressman Ted Weiss on the West Side of Manhattan (Hunter was on the East Side, and still is), but I must share a quick couple of stories about my time doing polls.

There was an older man also working the public opinion polls with whom I became friends. He was about 55 at the time and was a very nice, sweet man who was a struggling actor. I asked why he was doing these polls and he told me he had nothing—no retirement savings, no health insurance, no nothing. He had no family and no financial future to look forward to. He was frightened and I felt terrible for him. He told me not to let this happen to me. I've always remembered that tale. There was also a pretty young redhead there that I was attracted to but she seemed to have a boyfriend. A handsome young man, they were always hanging around together. I became friends with them both and finally learned they were *both* gay. I discovered this in a conversation with her when I asked her out on a date and she said she was gay and he was bisexual and they were *definitely not* an item, just friends. When I (still learning) said, "Bisexual?" she responded, "He just loves people." That line has never left me.

Since I had been a high school intern, I was familiar with internships. Hunter College had an intern program too except you still had to go to class. But I saw an opening with a *very* liberal Democratic West Side Congressman and jumped at the chance. The work was fun it was politics and social work doing "constituent service" and cutting red tape when people had trouble with government agencies (like missing Social Security checks, something with which I could sympathize). I was very enthusiastic about the work and became close with the staff. I worked many more hours than the internship required and generally made myself useful. I got to meet the Congressman and he was delightful to speak with. All in all, a great experience!

When the internship ended after one semester, they offered me a part-time job doing the same work but with more responsibility. It didn't take me more than one second to say, "Yes." I even had to sign (as part of the new hire papers) the oath of office—to swear to preserve, protect and defend the Constitution. It was a very proud moment for me!

I spent two years in the office as a part time staffer. The office was directly across from Lincoln Center, a block from Central Park. I was right in the middle of Manhattan, east side, west side, all around the town! I was still working at WNYU radio during this time—my love of radio remained— and I was a full-time college student. Life was busy! I spent a lot of time on the subways and buses getting around the city but found some time to socialize, especially on Friday nights in Greenwich Village (where WNYU was located) and weekends when I wasn't studying. I went to Met and Yankee games; all manner of things. I even tried my hand at ice skating with a girlfriend at a rink near Madison Square Garden. Boy, did my ankles hurt! I walked around a lot and would often walk by the Waldorf-Astoria and think, "That's where the rich people stay. I'll never get to stay there." (One day I did, as a lawyer, on a return trip to New York with my wife Frances—it was sweet!)

In contrast to the six years in the residences, those college years went fast. My grades were excellent, and I was thinking about my career more and more as time went by. I had a lot of friends at Hunter and enjoyed my time there immensely. The classes were fun and challenging, and I was growing up. One of the staffers in Congressman Weiss' office envisioned a political career for me in New York City. I was appreciative but said I wanted to move away. During this time, the late 1970s and 1980, New York was a *disaster*. The city had gone bankrupt and been taken over by the state. Homeless people were everywhere. De-institutionalization had started, just as Governor Carey had promised, except instead of building halfway houses for the people cooped up in the horrible state hospitals, they were dumped into the street. The subways were rolling hell. Crime was rampant. Because I was poor, and with my background, in that place, at that time, I had one idea: Get me the hell out of here! Plus, the new mayor, Ed Koch (pronounced kotch—not like the Koch—pronounced coke—brothers) was consciously changing Manhattan by forcing poor people out and giving away huge tax benefits to developers to "rehab" buildings and bring the rich in. And this dude was a Democrat! I saw what he was doing—my specialty in Congressman Weiss' office was local housing issues. Ed Koch was re-shaping the housing market and creating a lot of displaced and homeless old folks in the process. Combined with everything I had seen growing up, was seeing then, and had been living through, I had seen more than enough of New York City and *really* wanted out!

My career choice was disc jockey or lawyer. I absolutely *loved* radio—the whole of it—the people, the news writing, working the knobs and switches on the board, being on the air, sitting around listening to music and shooting the breeze with my friends. It was very exciting and I enjoyed working on getting rid of my accent, to sound better on the air. I was told by one of the guys to read the newspaper into a tape recorder and listen back—the accent would be obvious and the words that made it obvious would be even more obvious. So I did. I read *The New York Times* into a simple little tape recorder and listened back. I became much more conscious of my enunciation and worked consciously to change the way I spoke. It seemed to work well enough. After five years working at WNYU, I knew I was totally hooked on radio. I wanted very much to make a career out of it, but I saw the industry instability and was hesitant about putting all my career eggs in the radio basket.

I had a career choice to make. I knew enough after these several years working at WNYU and observing the radio industry to know that the life of a disc jockey was itinerant. Six months in one place, fired and then hired for 12 months somewhere else far away, and so on. I figured this would be fun for a short time as I envisioned doing overnights in Ft. Lauderdale, Florida, playing Emerson, Lake and Palmer records then getting off work at dawn, going to the beach, smoking a joint and watching the sunrise. I quickly realized, however, that one could only do that for so long before getting old and the routine getting boring. Also, having spent my entire life broke, I thought it would be wise to choose a career that would enable me to make a nice living. This would be *especially* true if I got married and had kids and needed to provide for a family. So I decided that, as much as I loved radio, it would be far more responsible and forward-thinking to be a lawyer.

I formulated a plan at the end of my junior year and before starting my senior year in college: Go to law school somewhere far away. Leave the city and go to law school. It seemed my best way out of the New York City madhouse. But I would need financial help and *I really* needed a rest. I was tired from all the things I was doing, all the things I had been through in life to that point (I was only 21) and I was tired of being a student. So I approached the Congressman and his staff with a proposal: After graduation, hire me full-time. I would work for a year and use that year to get ready for law school. Then I would leave and they could plan for their staffing knowing what my plans were. To my delight and surprise, they said, "Super—done deal!" So I was able to make a little more money for that last year in New York than I had on the Social Security-and-VA-benefits-plus-part-time-jobs program (Social Security was about $300 per month, the VA was always $24 and the part-time jobs were a few hundred). The Congressman paid me $1,000 a month working full-time, so I was doing all right!

College graduation was a blast, getting college behind me felt good, and I liked knowing I'd have a year off from school. I settled into full-time work in the Congressman's office and started looking for law schools. On Christmas Day (literally,) I typed my group of law school applications on a used IBM

Selectric electric typewriter that I had bought cheap to write my college papers. Christmas Day was my mother's birthday and the symbolism was not lost on me. It was December 25, 1981 and I was both excited and scared about moving away and going to law school. It was an intimidating idea, but I was determined and pushing myself through the fear. I spoke with the staff at the Congressman's office. We were all good friends by then and they knew my background. I told them I was concerned about putting my "poor orphan boy" story on the law school applications, but they told me that since it was the truth and I *would* need financial help that I should push past that concern and write it down. So I did!

There was a service which, for a small fee, would give a basic version of your grades and life story to a large pool of law schools. The law schools that were interested would write back saying, "Based on what we see here, if the rest looks like this, we'll accept you." I paid the fee and put my little application in. I got back a positive letter from the University of Toledo (Ohio) law school and a law school in Brooklyn. I cannot remember which one, but once I saw "Brooklyn" I said, "Forget it." However, I was *very* happy to know that *some* law school, somewhere, would take me, and that my dream of being a lawyer might actually come true! I just kept thinking about my parents and my beginnings and kept telling myself, "Dare to dream and keep working hard!"

I finally settled on six law schools, all in California. I looked at and eliminated New Mexico, Arizona, Florida, plus all the other warm weather states and said, "I'm going to *California*." I had never been west of Philadelphia, but what the hell. I was going to leap before I looked! I chose three California schools in the northern part of the state and three in the southern. Of those six, three were "safety" schools and three were top notch. Stanford turned me down immediately. All I could do was laugh. I mailed the applications package on a Monday morning. The next Monday evening when I got home from work, the rejection letter was there! It went from New York to Palo Alto (outside of San Francisco). They must have opened it and *immediately* said, "No way" and put the rejection letter in the mail *that same day* in order for it to get back to me the following Monday. A new land speed record! My law school application career was off to a great start!

I was turned down for my top three schools—Stanford, the University of California at Berkeley and USC—although I made the waiting list at USC before being told, "No." I was, however, accepted at all my safety schools—McGeorge School of Law in Sacramento (where Supreme Court Justice Anthony Kennedy was connected); California Western School of Law in San Diego; and Loyola Marymount in Los Angeles. The best (as far as I could tell) of the three safety schools was Loyola. While I had told all six schools I was poor and would need financial help, I did not over emphasize that fact. I was simply direct and matter of fact about it. Having zeroed in on Loyola, I wrote to them with a real heavy pitch of poverty and said I would need every bit of help I could get to attend. A few weeks later, they sent me a letter (no e-mails in *those* days; there were barely any fax machines around) offering me a full tuition scholarship, if I kept my grades in the top 20% of my class. I jumped so high, I think I could have dunked a basketball on Julius Erving! *I was going to California!*

Fortunately, one of the kids I was in the Pleasantville Cottage School with and had remained friends with after we both got a bit older, had moved to Los Angeles a year before me. He worked for a big department store chain that transferred him out there to help the sales staff in L.A. When

I was applying to schools, he and I had spoken over the year about my potentially joining him out there, and it had come to pass! I now knew I had a tour guide and someone to share an apartment with so I would not be going to Los Angeles completely alone.

In the days leading up to the move, I was a wreck. I had never been so scared in my life, before or since. This was a huge move and I was wracked with self-doubts and fear. But the day came—July 17, 1982—and off to the airport I went. A one way ticket to LAX (Los Angeles International Airport). On take-off from JFK Airport in New York, I looked out the window and saw Far Rockaway and the whole city stretched out before me, and felt like I had conquered the place. I had *survived*—and even prospered just a little—and I was damn proud of myself. A new world waited!

* * * * *

"I wouldn't want to belong to any club that would have me as a member." —Groucho Marx

PART
2
LAW AND RADIO

7

LOS ANGELES
AND LAW SCHOOL

My friend picked me up at LAX and drove us to his small apartment. We were going to get a larger one, but at least I had a place to stay! I had exactly one month to get a car, figure out how to get to law school and get acclimated to the city as best I could. His apartment was very close to the Hollywood sign; that was a nice touch. I had gotten my driver's license six months earlier, at age 22, knowing the last thing I would have time for in L.A. was to learn to drive. So I did it in New York and just exchanged the licenses in L.A. I had never had a need for a driver's license in New York City (where the hell was I going, and did I have money for a car?). I was always too busy and didn't have money to be going around traveling. Vacation? What's a vacation?

I bought a cheap used car from a dealer in Pasadena and found the law school was only a short drive away from my new home. A short drive *without traffic*, that is. L.A. traffic quickly let me know that being a commuter has its downsides. But my attitude was, "Hey, it's *not* the subway, I have my own personal space and I have an FM radio and my freedom." So I was happy!

The first day of law school was orientation. Each student stood up and spoke 30 seconds about him or herself. We were in a huge lecture hall; there had to have been 130 students in there. We got the standard, "Look to your right, look to your left; one of you won't be here at the end of the year." I had heard about that—and it happened that first day! And you know what? *It's true!* That lecture hall (where we took all our classes that first year) was a lot roomier by the end of that year. Of course, for my part, there was no "Plan B." I was *not* going to be one of the dropouts.

During the time I spent working in Queens Borough Hall and the Hugh Carey campaign and the Congressman's office, I had gotten to know quite a few lawyers. Some of them just weren't impressive, intellectually speaking. While I did not share my thoughts with these guys, I told myself, "If *these* guys can be lawyers, I can be on the Supreme Court," and that thought sustained me. During the 30-second presentation each student made about him or herself, I found a *massively* diverse and talented class: A lot of women; a lot of people in their 30s and 40s; and even one guy who was 65, who had just gotten out of the Army and said, "I always wanted to go to law school." We all bonded quickly. I have friends to this day from that law school class.

I had been telling myself, for at least a couple of years before moving to L.A., "Norm, you'll be 23 when you start law school. You can be a full-fledged attorney at *26 years-old.* When you're 30, law school will seem a distant memory, but you will wake up *every day the rest of your life* benefiting from the three years you busted your ass in that law school. It's worth the investment in yourself." I held onto that thought.

I started Loyola in August 1982 and graduated in May 1985. It was some of the most fun I have had in my life. Law school was an absolute *blast*! Sure, the first year is tough—there is a ton of reading—but it was absolutely fascinating reading! I found myself mumbling "fascinating" (just like Mr. Spock from *Star Trek*) as I was reading the case books. The intellectual stimulation was amazing. The eye-opening topics, the pushing of your mind—it was thrilling! And a lot of it was politics; the same stuff I knew, just from a different angle. There was Congress, there was the President, there were the states and all of this law stuff was just politics from a different angle. I ate it up! I finished around the tenth percentile all three years and graduated a bit outside the tenth percentile. I had law clerk jobs that showed me how the guts of the legal system worked. It didn't make the best impression on me, but there was a lot of work around and it was a good way to make a living.

There was a problem. I had thought about going to law school to enable me to return to politics and work in Washington, D.C. I had never considered staying in law and actually *practicing* it. My goal was to write the bill to nationalize Exxon, and I wanted to do it as a member of Senator Ted Kennedy's staff. I flew to Washington shortly after graduation where Ted Weiss was kind enough to set up interviews for me with various members of Congress. Ted had no openings but was very helpful in making introductions for me. As I made the rounds of the halls of Congress, I got this sick feeling in my stomach. I was having doubts as to whether I really wanted to do this. It was 1985. Ronald Reagan was riding high, and I remembered the politicians I had known earlier and recalled that they weren't always the best of people. I was wondering whether I wanted to be deep in the bowels of the political system and, if it didn't work out, I would be trapped and stuck with no legal experience. I was beginning to think that flexibility is important and to have that, I needed to practice the law for awhile. All these thoughts were happening *as I was interviewing all over Capitol Hill.* Finally, during these interviews, Dan Rostenkowski, a powerful Congressman from Chicago, offered me a job on the House Ways and Means Committee staff. This is a *major* plum job. The Ways and Means Committee writes tax laws. A staffer can master the tax code or select pieces of it, then go off and earn whopping sums of money selling that knowledge to any and every corporation and rich person in America. The tax code is a labyrinth; master it and you have the keys to the Washington, D.C. financial empire. And Congressman Rostenkowski wanted me to start *Monday.* It was Wednesday. I said, "You mean *this coming* Monday?" He said, "Yeah, what's the problem?" I said, "I wanted to go back to California, pass the Bar exam, get my license and start in August or so." He said, "But I need you *now.* You flew here all the way from California to get this job—it's a good job—do you want the job or not?"

At that moment I saw it all—the future in two paths, and I was standing at the fork in the road. If I took the Rostenkowski path, I would be a staffer and then I would have a career as a tax lawyer. If I went back to California, I would take the Bar exam and practice. I knew that if I didn't practice soon after passing the Bar and later needed a job practicing (to support myself or my family), it would be very difficult. I would be competing against kids like myself who would work cheaper and longer hours. I would have to explain why I had never taken a deposition; never done a jury trial or written an appeal brief. And I had to choose—right then. I said, "Thanks so much for the opportunity, but I'm just not able to move here in a few days' time." He shook his head, shook my hand and wished me the best. I could read his mind: "What an asshole," and I was kind of agreeing with him! I went back to L.A. and passed the Bar exam the first try.

I decided that I was going to change course. I would practice law for awhile, get the skills needed to be a practicing lawyer, and then decide whether to go back into politics. My original plan—for a three-year stay in California, followed by a return to politics in the nation's capital—was going to be extended. I had fallen in love with Los Angeles, California and the West. I traveled some and saw all the beauty of the Rocky Mountains and many of the other states west of the Rockies. The Grand Canyon was my favorite spot on Earth—not that I had seen many spots on Earth. It was all spectacular and I felt at home and comfortable in Los Angeles in a way I had never felt at home in New York.

And there was another problem. I didn't know what to do; what legal field to go into. This turned out to be a big mistake. I didn't have a plan. I didn't know what type of law to practice. Some types of law (like litigation) are very stressful; others, like writing wills, not so much. I had not thought the matter through. I fell into a job and it was the *wrong* job. I had worked as a law clerk for a very large firm and then for a solo practitioner. I learned that litigation was bustling and had a lot of jobs available. I decided to work for the solo practitioner. It would be a way to get into the cases deeply and quickly. Most young lawyers at big firms spent two years writing dull research memos. They're stuck long hours in a law library and essentially doing briefcase-carrying duties for more senior lawyers, and I did not want to do that! I wanted to take the depositions, do the trials, and get into the courtrooms. This was my way.

The solo practitioner was a very difficult person to work for—no mentoring and lots of yelling. He assumed I knew what

I was doing, as if I was an experienced attorney, and it was sink or swim in the deep end of the pool. I learned, but at great psychological cost. It was grueling and very stressful and the money was bad. Even with a scholarship and part-time jobs, I was deeply in debt but I was getting into the courtroom and into depositions and into all manner of situations that brand new lawyers never get into. I was right in the guts of the legal system. Here I was, a brand new attorney and I was doing it all—in the courtroom, arguing cases, writing briefs and in way over my head! I was getting no mentoring; I was being baffled by the system; it was far too complex; there were too many formalities and rules and far too much greed and lying and I was not reacting well to it at all. I did not have time to prepare; I was getting too much work thrown at me. I hated the judges, the other lawyers and their games, and the sheer stupidity of a system that delivered no justice but certainly transferred lots of money into the pockets of the lawyers running the system. I hated the insurance companies that were playing the system. Let's face it, I was hating it all.

I hashed it out for a couple of years (I can be a stubborn mule) and became burnt out, cynical and hateful. I quit. I tried doing work on my own for a year but that didn't work either. I couldn't get good clients and didn't know how to do it anyway. My money troubles grew. I went back to work for that solo practitioner lawyer I had worked for and it only got worse. After another year of that, I quit again. I ran into more money troubles. I got suspended from the Bar for a few months for not paying my Bar dues. Not that it mattered to me at that point. I wasn't practicing much and my attitude was so awful, I really didn't care. I was in a deep depression. Here I was nearly 30 years old, a lawyer for three years, a total mess, depressed, second guessing myself, and broke. I had been living hand to mouth, working for hourly wages and just squeaking by. That great plan I had years earlier had veered *seriously* off track. I was in deep trouble, personally and professionally. I was berating myself. After all that time and all the setbacks and all the work to be at rock bottom. I was contemplating suicide. It was *that* bad. The period of 1986 to 1990 was a very bad time.

* * * * *

8
FRANCES

My brother Ron was getting married in June 1990 in a little town outside Columbus, Ohio. He asked me to be the best man. I quickly and gratefully agreed. I called a friend who was a sportswriter and said, "I'll be in the Midwest. Let's meet up and go watch baseball games and drink heavily." He thought that was a great idea so I scraped up some money and away I went to the wedding outside Columbus, then off to Chicago. On the plane on the way to Cleveland, my friend told me we would be meeting a woman there. She lived near me in Los Angeles. He had been trying to get us to meet for eight years, but it just never worked out. She was from Cleveland and was visiting her family. On June 15, 1990, a beautiful spring day in Cleveland, I met Frances.

This friend met Frances while visiting me in L.A. in 1982, shortly after I moved there. He was starting a graduate program at Stanford and moved to Northern California at the same time I moved to Southern California. He went to law school with me one day—had enough of *that*—and spent the next few days going around L.A. with my roommate, who had a friend who knew Frances. My friend spent the next eight years trying to get us to meet. Frances and I literally lived a mile and a half apart. It just never happened, until we landed in Cleveland on June 15, 1990.

I first set eyes on Frances at the Cleveland-Hopkins Airport by the baggage claim area. She was very pretty. I kicked myself for not meeting her during the past eight years. My friend kept *trying* to get us to meet; another mistake I made! We all went to the baseball game. Frances and I spent a lot of time talking about politics; we had the same views. I told her of my bitterness in the legal system and she (while not a lawyer) was very sympathetic. We both loved baseball. I fell in love with her talking at the Cleveland Municipal Stadium, watching the Cleveland Indians and being surprised at how nice Cleveland was. It was my first trip there and I was expecting a bombed-out shell of a city, kind of like London 1944. To the contrary, Cleveland had been rebuilt and no one seemed to know it.

I fell in love with Cleveland, Frances, and the Indians, all at the same time. Frances was great—smart and sweet, yet sharp and tough. She was well educated and we spoke a lot about a lot of topics with politics chief among them. When I got back to Los Angeles, I called her and we were married five months later. On August 10th, she was already introducing me as her fiancée so it didn't take long for us to figure out that we should be together. And I became an Indians fan and remain one to this day. (I had not had a team since leaving New York and was disgusted with George Steinbrenner, who was from Cleveland, destroying the Yankees and making it all about *his* ego.)

It is not overstating it to say Frances saved my life. She gave me new energy, love and support. She helped me dig out of my financial troubles and encouraged me to get another law job at a law firm where I could actually learn by being mentored, and

I did. I got a good job at a big law firm and it turned out that all that crazy time I had spent with the solo practitioner had actually drilled a bunch of good stuff into my legal head. I was actually a better lawyer than I thought! What I had needed to do was calm down and not hate the system so much. I needed to master it and to, as some describe President Obama, "Play chess." I got my legs under me and stabilized, both as a lawyer and as a person. I made friends at this law firm. I calmed down and dug into the legal system. Instead of flailing, I was now working smoothly. I'm a relatively quick learner and I absorbed a lot, and a lot of what I had previously experienced fell into place. Things started to make more sense. Frances' family (which was large) was very good to me. My new father-in-law was a wonderful man who became like a second father to me. He also loved politics, was a true Democrat, and we spent a lot of time debating. Even though we often agreed, we argued just for the sake of arguing, and that made Frances laugh and yell at us simultaneously!

After 18 months at the big law firm, I moved to a medium-sized law firm. The partners there liked me a lot; they gave me great responsibilities and great support. I gained confidence and handled ever-higher profile cases, and got good results. By the time 1995 rolled around, I was ready to go on my own. Looking back, it was a really rough way to get going (and I would *not* recommend it to anyone—nor would I do it over again if I could avoid it) but it *did* have a pattern of progression to it. I started with car accidents and moved up the complexity chain to bigger and more complex cases.

I started my own little law office on Hollywood Boulevard on March 1, 1995, just a couple of blocks from the famous Chinese Theater (with all the handprints and footprints in the cement in front) and actually did pretty well. By that time, I had handled complex cases, done some trials and now moved into class action lawsuits. From that time until returning to radio, I handled California class action lawsuits and other complex litigation, and despite still hating the legal system—more precisely, the people and institutions in it—I managed to make a good living and do the public some good by suing bad corporate players who were taking advantage of consumers.

* * * * *

9
SUMMARY OF THE
LEGAL SYSTEM

I can now report that the legal system is a disgrace. After working as a law clerk, young lawyer, mid-level lawyer and big case lawyer and seeing *lots* of judges, insurance companies, big corporations and other lawyers, the system is rotten to the core. The judges are politicians in robes. They don't even try to hide their biases anymore. They are appointed to the bench to advance a political agenda and advance they do! The lawyers—*especially* the corporate trial lawyers—routinely hide evidence; lie to the judges; lie to their fellow lawyers; and break every ethical rule in the business. They hide or deny the existence of documents; they deny evidence exists when it does (such as where witnesses can be found); and they tell witnesses to lie. It's called "suborning perjury." They force their opponents (like me) to go around them and expose the truth. This gets expensive and time consuming. Private investigators are not cheap. Also, the amount of time I and other lawyers like me have to spend exposing their lies is a disincentive to fight. Many lawyers in my position simply won't go through the aggravation we're put through by the corporate trial lawyers and their corporate employers. They throw in the towel or settle cheap, thereby rewarding the unethical conduct and encouraging more of it. Even when consumer protection lawyers are diligent and stubborn, invest the time and money to dig, and expose the lying and cheating, and *show* the corporate trial lawyers lied and were caught red-handed, they get away with it. I've exposed them several times and know a lot of my fellow consumer protection attorneys who have done likewise. The judges just shrug it off as part of the process. Knowing that all manner of unethical behavior is acceptable, the corporate trial lawyers continue to do it and their corporate employers reward them for it with more business.

Many large corporate law firms groom their lawyers to be judges and, once on the bench, they continue to advance the corporate agenda. "The law" as a body of rules—past precedent and established procedures—means little or nothing. Those prior cases, precedent supposedly to be followed, are ignored, "distinguished" on ridiculous grounds or simply overturned. The powerful pay their lawyers to abuse the system and their lawyers abuse it with impunity. They delay and obfuscate, and the judges bring no justice to the system. I blame the judges. They can clean it up in a short time by disciplining the lawyers (and their clients) who abuse the system, but they don't. I never liked the system in its entirety, the lying and cheating aside. It is *extremely* slow and inefficient. It is prohibitively expensive to bring a case forward. The lawyers charge too much (especially the corporate trial lawyers); the judges rig the game for the corporations; and the victims of negligence or corporate abuse don't receive nearly the measure of recompense they deserve after deductions for court costs and legal fees. Because the costs of running a case are so high (a short, routine deposition can cost a lawyer $1,000) and the consumer protection lawyers advance this money (the clients cannot afford this) when the case resolves, the client sees a big chunk of money go to the lawyer as simple reimbursement of costs advanced, and the client is unhappy. Of course, the corporate trial lawyers forced many of these expenses to be incurred by dragging the case out and forcing the consumer protection lawyers to go on wild goose chases.In the end, the client is simply angry at having to wait so long and get so little.

The "Republicon" Party has so politicized the court system that getting a fair hearing is extremely difficult. My bitterness with the legal system comes from looking at it from the public's standpoint. I never accepted that it was all a giant money sharing game and I was on the inside, there to simply carve up the pie and take my big slice of it. I always made noise about the corrupt and inefficient nature of the system *to* the system and I was looked at as crazy. Why not just shut up and take my share? I couldn't stomach it anymore and was weary from the whole experience. It was time to move on.

* * * * *

THE RETURN TO RADIO

After becoming a lawyer and practicing for the many years I slogged through it—disliking almost all of it—I had one of those "light bulb going on over the head" moments and thought about my love for radio and returning to it. It happened in 2002. The reason it happened was because I had moved my office into a building close to home that was full of studios—recording studios. I saw the people working in them and they reminded me of my radio days and my love of radio. I realized that, by acquiring a lot of experience in the bowels of the legal profession, I could use that knowledge to either be a lawyer *on* the radio or a political commentator with a lawyer theme on the radio. I kicked myself that I had not thought of this sooner, but figured that later is better than never.

Having not been on the radio for over 20 years, I knew I needed to knock the rust off and get behind a microphone again. Fortunately, I had become friends with a few of the people in the building where I did my law work, and spoke with them about renting their studios when they were not using them. Again, fortunately, two guys who had a group of studios were helpful and let me use their studios for no charge when they weren't using them. They even asked one of their engineers to help me, and he did. We also became friends. In fact, this engineer, let's call him "Mick" (not his real name) was in his late 50s and had been in radio and engineering his whole working life. When I told him of my radio days in the middle and late 1970s and early 1980s, he laughed as we discussed the now-primitive equipment used in those days: the huge, reel-to-reel tape machines where editing was done with a single-edged razor blade and an editing "block" of raised metal. It was about five inches side-to-side and three inches top-to-bottom on the front of the tape machine. The block had a diagonal slit in the middle and a groove running side-to-side in the middle. You would thread the tape in the groove and when you got to the right spot, slice the tape in the two places it needed editing and then use adhesive tape to patch the two ends together. You had better get it right the first time! You would listen to the tape through the speakers in the studio. The noise, as you manually slowly moved the tape back and forth, would make strange sounds.

In those days, we had "cart machines" which were literally 8-track tape deck-looking things with what certainly looked like 8-track tapes playing in them. They were used for recorded commercials and "PSAs" (public service announcements) as well as other material. We had "bulk erase" machines where you would turn on the thing (it was the size of a small shoe box, about five pounds in weight, and would make a loud, annoying sound when turned on) and rub the 8-track cartridges over the top metal plate. In theory, that would erase the material on the 8-track so you could record new material on it. Of course, if you didn't erase thoroughly enough and then recorded over it, you had two different recordings overlapping on the tape and it would make the oddest sounds.

Nowadays all of this is done on computers with digital abilities. You can do all manner of things to audio while preserving the original in case you make mistakes. At least the microphones, headphones and sound control boards look the same! Mick brought me up to date on what happened in the intervening 20 years while I was practicing law and the radio and recording industry went through the technological revolution. It turned out I missed a lot. Shortly after I left the industry for law school, computers were introduced. But there were problems. The computers were primitive; they failed; they locked up; they just stopped and the employees were pulling their hair out. Just as I was re-entering the field in 2002, computers were settling down and getting quite reliable. I was glad I missed all of *that*!

I was nervous the first time I got behind the microphone back in 2002. It had been so long! I was actually sweating, even though we were recording a three-minute little political commentary that was going nowhere—not to be broadcast anywhere—just for me to listen to for cadence and accent and the like. Nevertheless, I was very nervous. I got through that and began recording more of these little pieces and getting professionals to critique me. One guy, who was down the hall and a former disc jockey, worked for a radio syndication company (they got radio shows on radio stations). Let's call him "Jay" (not his real name). He was very helpful in getting me to sound more conversational and smooth. We talked radio show technique and the way to handle a talk radio show from a host's perspective. It turned out that Jay was from Minnesota, worked in Fargo, North Dakota and knew who Ed Schultz was. It's a small world!

I did all this while still practicing the law. I tried to fit in the radio stuff as much as I could, given the time constraints. That's when I met our current engineer, Kozz—which *is* his real name—and we began working together in Kozz's studio, also in the same building. It was 2003 and into early 2004. I finally decided that I needed to get back on the *actual radio airwaves* to see if I could make a go of this potential career change. But getting on local radio in Los Angeles was not easy then or now, and there was no radio station that played my brand of politics on its airwaves. I would have to improvise.

On weekends all over the radio dials of America, people pay money to put their radio shows on the air. It's called "brokered time" and how much it costs depends upon what time slot you buy and what city or town you are in, as well as how strong a signal the radio station has. In a small city, if you buy an undesirable time, it can cost as little as one or a few hundred dollars for a slot (the length of time is up for negotiation). But in a big city like Los Angeles, the second largest radio market in America (New York is first), the FM talk radio station I targeted was cost prohibitive. (Howard Stern was on in the mornings before he went to satellite.) The high cost was especially true since I wanted a desirable Saturday morning slot. I negotiated with the radio station and we made a deal—an expensive one—but I got to use their facilities, meet their people and get a big signal for my voice in a slot where I could be reasonably assured a bunch of people would be listening. I bought an hour, from 10:00 a.m. to 11:00 a.m. on Saturday mornings, beginning in mid-June 2004 and running until right up to the election—the Bush versus Kerry presidential election.

Most of the brokered time you'll hear on the radio is clearly commercial time—people selling real estate advice, doing yoga classes, chiropractors, gardening shows, all manner of things where they want you to "come on down" and do business with them. They're pushing their regular business. For them it's advertising. My hour stood out since I was doing a "liberal" talk radio hour and didn't want to sell anything but a philosophy. Of course, if I got a case referral or two out of it (but I did not) then that would be ok, too! That hour did indeed get a lot of attention and, for whatever it was worth, we did get the highest ratings on that station on weekends. It was largely because people had their pre-set buttons to that station for Howard Stern, and when they got into their cars on Saturday mornings to do their errands, they turned on the radio and there I was—talking politics! We got a lot of phone calls and I enjoyed the time immensely. I got better week-by-week and got critiqued by people (a now expanding group of friends) as the weeks progressed. I got to use sound clips and take calls. After spending many hours with Mick and Kozz and getting critiqued by Jay, in 2003 and the first half of 2004, the hours on Saturdays in the summer of 2004 helped get me back in radio shape. I was hooked on radio all over again! I remembered how much fun it was and how I enjoyed the entire process: putting a show together, the preparation, the excitement of being on the air, the people, being fascinated by how the equipment worked—all of it.

Since I got to spend time at the radio station, I got to know some of the people there. One in particular was a very nice guy who happened to share my politics. Let's call him "Don" (not his real name) who was quite high up in the station management. A couple of weeks into the show, he said, "Norm, we have a couple of extra press passes to the Democratic National Convention in Boston. You would have to pay your own way but if you want to get in, I can give you a pass." He didn't have to ask me twice! I arranged for a hotel room (it was literally right next to Fenway Park) and flights and was ready to go! Frances didn't go with me as I couldn't get her a pass and she said it would be way too hectic and I would be working long hours, so I should just go alone—she was right! I flew out on Sunday morning and that night in the hotel, I could hear Fenway Park roaring. John Kerry was in the front row and the Red Sox were playing! I was watching on television; it must have been a great night for Senator Kerry.

I went with a reporter's pass and thus brought a radio station-issued digital recorder (we called them tape recorders in the old days), and threw myself into the craziness of a political convention! Recall that this was 2004. This was the John Kerry-John Edwards convention. The Iraq invasion and occupation were happening; George W. Bush had proven to be the anti-Christ I feared he would be; and "liberal" talk radio was just getting started. By that time, I had XM Satellite radio and, in early January 2004, heard this guy Ed Schultz on the radio. At first I thought he was Rush Limbaugh (the voices sounded similar) but the content was *vastly* different. Also, the *Los Angeles Times* did a front page story on Ed right after the New Year 2004, and I read that story with alacrity. By the time of the Convention, I had been listening to Ed regularly and liked him a lot. He and Air America (which started a couple of months after Ed went on the air.; being separately syndicated, Ed was never a part of Air America) were getting a good amount of attention—if not radio stations—and I was eager to see if I could join their ranks. By this time, the summer of 2004, I was determined to switch careers and get back into radio doing "liberal" or "progressive" talk.

On Monday morning, first day of the Convention, I went to the press briefing and while standing on the side (all the chairs had been taken by the time I got there), I noticed Helen Thomas in the front row. Having been a political junkie my whole life, I had watched countless presidential news conferences with her always in front and invariably getting the first question. She was a real pain in the butt of every president (George W. Bush had stripped her of her front row seat and disrespected her greatly), and a legend in the political reporting field. She was her usual self that Monday morning, asking great and uncomfortable questions and not taking silly answers lightly. I waited for the briefing to end and then walked up to her. I introduced myself and we started talking. A young reporter also started talking with her and there the three of us stood, chatting amicably in the press briefing room. I was in heaven! Then after a few minutes, Ms. Thomas invited us both to breakfast. I instantly said, "Yes!" The three of us went to the hotel coffee shop. Ms. Thomas could not have been more gracious, more kind, more helpful or friendly. She was delightful—funny, energetic, full of stories and I was absolutely enthralled! It was a long breakfast and the three of us had a grand time.

The young reporter of our group had to leave, but after breakfast Ms. Thomas invited me along to *the floor* of the Convention. She was, of course, instantly recognized by everyone and had access wherever she wanted to go. The fact that I was next to her meant that I, too, got to go everywhere and it was great! We made the rounds, meeting lots of well-known politicians and political journalists, and then found ourselves at the lectern on the stage on the Convention floor, from where all the speeches were made. And standing there was Governor Bill Richardson of New Mexico, who was one of the key people organizing and running the Convention. It was here that I stuck my microphone in his face and asked, "What does the Democratic Party stand for?" He gave me a bad answer, staring off into space, letting many seconds uncomfortably trickle by. He then looked at me and said, "Unions? Women's rights?" then stopped talking and looked at me like I was an idiot.

Ms. Thomas kept me by her side all that morning and early afternoon and then finally said she had to get back to her bureau office (in a building a few blocks away) to write her column. I bid her a fond farewell and she left me with a few lasting favors: I now knew where the press section was, it was directly behind the lectern on the floor and a very nice place to watch the Convention, and she showed me how to get in that section by using the press pass with security. I made sure I made good mental notes. Those lessons stood me in very good stead throughout the days of the Convention.

I never did see Helen Thomas again after that morning. A few years later, she got herself into a heap of trouble for saying that Israel should not exist (she is of Lebanese descent), and that episode forced her into retirement. I was saddened to hear her remarks—being Jewish and a supporter of Israel—but she had to have known my religion given I introduced myself and there was my press pass hanging around my neck with my name in bold and plain view. To me, she was as sweet and nice a person as I have ever met, and while I certainly do not agree with her attitude toward Israel, I will always have a tremendous amount of respect and affection for Helen Thomas as a woman in the days of journalism when there were *no* women and making her way to the very top of her profession without looking like an underwear model. She was smart and tough and worked hard, all to her very great credit. So, thank you, Helen Thomas for what you did for me and for women professionals everywhere!

The second day of the Convention, I met up with the people from the radio station I was on. They introduced me to a radio guy who worked behind the scenes in Los Angeles and was very well known there and in national radio circles. He and I hit it off quickly (his name is not Kyle Gerrity, but let's call him that) and after talking awhile he said, "Norm, you're one of those trial lawyers that the Republicans keep beating up on. John Edwards is about to be nominated for Vice President. You're smart and a quick thinker, so tomorrow, let's have you put away your tape recorder, and you and I will walk up and down Radio Row and I'll get you booked on radio shows as the *interviewee* to defend the trial lawyers." I said, "Sure, sounds like fun," and off we went. "Radio Row" is the name given to the tables from where everyone broadcasts their shows. They're simple card tables covered with cloth, all lined up very close to each other, up and down hallways everywhere. Cables and microphones and technical equipment are jammed in; it's a lot of activity and people in a very small space.

Kyle called my cell phone every few minutes, saying, "Show up at such-and-such a table at such-and-such a time." I must have been on seven or eight interviews that afternoon, many on local radio stations (like WWRL in New York, the new "liberal" station). The two of us roamed the halls for hours, with Kyle setting up interviews and me doing them. He was a great help!

One of the shows he booked me on was *The Ed Schultz Show*. It turned out he was one of the people who had helped launch Ed's show through a project called Democracy Radio, so he was able to get me on! It was there that I first met Ed and his producer, a young man named James Holm (that *is* his real name) and Ed introduced me to him as "Holmey," which I found ironic since he is a 6'2" blonde haired, blue-eyed Norwegian from North Dakota, and there are just not a lot of homeys there! They were at one end of Radio Row, and not in the best location.

I had been listening to Ed on XM for seven months and was excited to actually meet him. I knew he had been a right-wing talk show host so, before we went on the air, I had a chance to chat with Ed for a few minutes and asked him why he had switched. He told me the story of meeting Wendy, his wife, and his eyes being opened by her and a group of homeless veterans over baloney sandwiches at a shelter. Then we did the interview (I had called Frances, told her what was going on and she went outside and sat in the car listening on XM), and it went very well. Ed especially liked that I was feisty and said, "If the Republicans want to cap jury awards and damages, then why aren't we also capping corporate profits?" At the end of the interview, on the air, Ed said, "Hey, I like this guy, let's have him on again." As I was leaving after the interview, I gave my business cards to Ed and Holmey, wrote my cell and home phone numbers on them and said, "Call me anytime, I'll be glad to help any way I can." I didn't see them for the rest of the Convention, but was hopeful something positive would come of it.

That Convention was some of the most fun I have ever had, and it was extremely beneficial to my budding radio career. Since I now knew the ins and outs of the press pass and press world, I spent a lot of time in the press section directly behind the podium. This was prime seating, and I got to witness a little history. A young state senator from Illinois, a guy named Barack Obama (if you can imagine *that* name!) was being introduced to the heavy hitters of the national media that second day of the Convention. I was sitting there just a couple of rows from where Chris Wallace of Fox "Boobs" was ensconced, when an entourage of security and staff surrounding this young, tall fellow came calling. I got to witness the first meeting of Barack Obama and Chris Wallace. They exchanged pleasantries and that was all. Then State Senator Obama was trundled off to meet others in the press corps.

The night then-State Senator Obama (he was to be elected to the United States Senate the night John Kerry had the election stolen by George W. Bush, Karl W. Rove and the Ohio Secretary of State, Ken Blackwell, November 2, 2004) gave his very well-received speech at the Convention, I was in a seat behind the podium. That speech was already getting buzz even before he gave it. Everyone wanted to hear this dynamic young man, so I was pleased to be able to sit close and watch. He was as good in person as he was on television! I also got to see Jimmy Carter, Hillary Clinton and Bill Clinton give their speeches. I was so close behind them I could read the teleprompter right along with them, and see when and where they deviated from their scripts. It was great fun! Hillary and Bill each deviated from their scripts a lot, while Jimmy Carter barely budged from his. Throughout it all, I kept thinking of my parents and how far I had come from the rats and roaches, the public housing projects and the orphanages. It was quite a journey.

The night John Kerry gave his speech I was stuck way up in the rafters. *That* ticket was a tough one to get; the big-time press corps got priority seating over me. But for the most part, I was able to get prime seating for most of the speeches, and got to watch the behind-the-scenes action as speakers were shuttled onto the podium and off. A terrific Congresswoman named Stephanie Tubbs-Jones from Cleveland gave a great speech, and I was able to get a picture of her right after she left the podium (she even stopped and chatted with me after the photo). She died in 2008 of a stroke. The Congress is poorer for her absence.

If you are a political junkie, it's fun to walk around these conventions because you run into *everyone* in the halls. Senators,

House members, big name journalists, they are all in this small, enclosed space and many of them are quite accessible. I enjoyed shaking hands with then-Senator Joe Biden and was able to see who was nice (Biden was) and who was not (Joe Lieberman was not), but I reminded myself that people's moods *do* change and maybe one person is nice at one moment and not nice the next. But I still don't like Joe Lieberman. Bill O'Reilly attracted quite a large crowd wherever he went, and he was just as much a jerk in person as on television. Writer/analyst Norman Ornstein was very nice and engaging to talk with. Those four days (the conventions run Monday through Thursday) were a terrific whirlwind of activity and helped me immensely.

I also ran into an old friend on the second night of the Convention, the *very guy* who got me into WNYU when I was 16 years-old. He was now working for Bloomberg Radio, covering the event. We went drinking that night and I stayed up until 4 a.m. with him and his co-workers, telling stories, catching up and drinking up a storm. I also ran into and chatted with Janeane Garofalo, and she was absolutely delightful! She was doing her show on Air America and the Air America table was a center of major activity. Lots of people wanted to meet and chat with the different personalities (Al Franken was there and got into a very spirited debate with Ted Koppel one day, surrounded by many people, me included) and I learned that the radio business, especially at the Conventions, is very incestuous. Many of the hosts would do interviews on the other hosts' shows, and then the other hosts would return the favors so that each host would be a guest on many other shows and host a bunch of other talk radio personalities on *their* show. Now *that's* incestuous!

While walking around Radio Row, getting interviews and being interviewed, I found myself standing directly behind

Janeane Garofalo as she was about to be interviewed live on Sean Hannity's radio show. I was a little creeped out to be that close to Hannity, but there was a big crowd and since I didn't want to throw up on anyone, especially Janeane's head, I kept my cool. Just as Janeane was about to go on the air with Hannity, I leaned over and whispered in her ear, "Janeane, ask Sean if smug, snotty and snide are family values." She busted out laughing, but didn't ask him. Well, she was the interviewee, not me! For my part, I would have asked, but I was not booked on Hannity's show.

This was actually my second Democratic National Convention. I was at the one in 1980 at Madison Square Garden in New York when Jimmy Carter was renominated, but ultimately lost to Ronald Reagan. I had supported Ted Kennedy in the primaries. He had challenged Jimmy Carter but came up short and as a consolation prize, the Carter people gave Kennedy one night of the Convention for his own. I was in the house that night. The Congressman I worked for at the time, Ted Weiss of New York, got me a ticket. It was thrilling to be a 21-year-old Congressional staffer and witness one of the greatest speeches of modern American political history. The audience was electric and the speech, which is available online, was so rousing that I, already a "veteran" of politics for six years, was cemented in as a political junkie that very night and I haven't stopped since.

❋ ❋ ❋ ❋ ❋

11
GETTING GOING ON THE ED SCHULTZ SHOW

After returning home from the Kerry-Edwards Convention in August 2004, I started getting calls from Holmey to be on the Ed Schultz Show via telephone to talk about the law. They asked for me to be in a quiet room and on a landline so that the sound quality was maximized. It happened that Scott Peterson was being tried for the murder of his wife Laci and their soon-to-be-born child. The trial ended in November and I was on with Ed to analyze the case several times. Later Michael Jackson was alleged to have molested a child at his home on the Neverland Ranch near Santa Barbara. I predicted Mr. Jackson would be acquitted and stuck with that as the trial progressed. Ed kept asking me about it and it turned out he *was* acquitted, so my stock rose quite a bit with Ed.

The thing about being a lawyer, especially one that has practiced awhile and kept up with the law, is that something is *always* happening in the legal world. There is *always* a new court case from somewhere that is noteworthy or newsworthy. There is *always* a trial that gets media attention. Congress is *always* debating a bill or passing a law that creates controversy. Some issue *always* arises that invites Constitutional analysis whether it is George W. Bush torturing prisoners at Guantanamo Bay or arresting Americans on American soil and holding them without charges or trial. Thus I found myself on the air with Ed a lot, and we began to speak together off the air and became friends. I found Ed to be a regular guy, friendly and with a lot of common sense and curiousity about the law. We developed a cordial relationship. I did my best to make myself accessible and available so that if breaking news happened, I could be on the air with Ed very quickly.

My own Saturday morning radio show ended on October 30, 2004. The election was the following Tuesday, and my only radio connection became being the lawyer on Ed's show. I loved doing it. Ed's show was growing and I was becoming a regular featured guest on the show. Ed told me off the air that he liked me *on the air* because I "didn't waste any words" and was able to explain the law in a way that a non-attorney could quickly grasp. I was glad to do it.

The following summer of 2005, I told Ed and Holmey that I had done my own show the summer I met them and would like to sub for Ed if he ever considered giving me a shot. I sent them some clips from my Saturday show and left it at that. By that time, Ed had been watching CNN enough to know that Jeffrey Toobin was billed as "The Senior Legal Analyst." One day on the air, Ed surprised me by saying, "You're being promoted—as of now you are our "Senior Legal Analyst," and we had great fun with that! From then on, Ed always hammed up the "Senior Legal Analyst" and I loved it—I adopted it both for the humor and the fun poked at CNN. I use that title to this day! The "Senior Legal Analyst" segments were on throughout 2004-2005 and into 2006. I had gotten very comfortable with Ed and being on the air.

Prior to my subbing for Ed, beginning on July 4, 2006, he used a variety of guest hosts and I liked most of them. One guy in particular, Peter B. Collins, was very good. He had a great radio voice and was a very smart commentator. Prior to my first subbing gig, I did not hound Ed or Holmey about guest hosting, but every once in a while I reminded them of my availability. I even told them I would fly to Fargo—at my own expense—and sit in Ed's chair, to make it easy for the staff to do their jobs.

For my part, I was curious about North Dakota—having never been there or anywhere *near* there—and wanted to give them an incentive to have me get a shot at hosting. They didn't seem all that interested. Whenever Ed took a day off, it was always some other host. I understood that I was not a big name like Jim Lampley, who subbed for Ed a fair bit, or Paul Hackett, an Iraq war veteran who made a splash by coming home and running for Congress on an anti-war platform and nearly defeating incumbent Republican Jean Schmidt in a Republican district near Cincinnati. I was not a long-time radio pro like Peter B. Collins, who had been on radio for years in San Francisco. So I contented myself being the lawyer on Ed's show and was happy to be doing that!

Then in May 2006, I got a call from Holmey asking if I was interested in hosting the show on Tuesday, July 4th, and if I was serious about the "coming to Fargo" thing. I said, "Yes" on all scores and got *very* excited! I later confirmed with Holmey that the reason I got my shot was because that year, 2006, July 4th was on a *Tuesday* and they couldn't get any other hosts to agree to do the show; it was a long weekend and no one wanted to break up their holiday. Ed wanted a live show on many days when other shows were running "Best Ofs" and that's how I got my chance!

I looked at the baseball schedule and the calendar and saw that the Twins were at home in Minneapolis that weekend playing the Brewers. Frances and I had a friend in Minneapolis so we planned a trip around the Fargo gig, with baseball and visiting on the weekend. Problem was, Frances had to be home during the week for her schedule. We worked out a plan where I dropped her off at the airport on Monday, July 3rd, and rented a car driving directly to Fargo, about a four-hour drive away.

We enjoyed the weekend in Minneapolis and had a great time at the baseball game. I got a Joe Mauer jersey and did the *Ed Schultz Show* wearing that jersey. I have a picture of it on the wall in our home office. So on Monday, July 3, 2006, we took a cab to the airport, I kissed Frances goodbye and rented a car for the drive north. As I said on the air during the Ed show the following day, Minnesota was the best *smelling* state I had ever been in. I rented a convertible—the weather was spectacular—and the drive from the Minneapolis airport to Fargo that afternoon was magnificent. Minnesota is a beautiful state and since I had never been there, I was taking it all in and enjoying every minute of it. I must confess I was nervous about doing the show the next day!

I met Holmey that evening in Fargo and we went over the show. Topic selection, how to begin the show, what advertisers we had "live reads" to do, and so forth. I learned that "formatics" is very important—getting into and out of breaks and handling the clock—and Holmey was very good at coaching. Ed was on a trip but the crew had agreed to work that day and work with *me*. I was thrilled! The next day we got into the studio early and the show went very well. Holmey was very pleased and the crew and I got along very well. As a joke, I ran a little contest and offered Ed's chair as the prize, then confessed I was joking since Ed would need a place to sit down upon his return. But it *was* a nice chair! We all went out for dinner and drinks afterwards and I was feeling ten feet tall! We even got a call on the air from a woman in the Los Angeles area who asked if I was the guy who had been on a couple of summers earlier on Saturday mornings. I said, "Indeed, it was me," and she said, "I wondered what happened to you—you were good," and that made me feel even better! The audience had gotten to know me from being the "Senior Legal Analyst" starting in the summer of 2004, so by the time I hosted for Ed that July 4, 2006, I had been on with Ed approximately 50 times, maybe more, I didn't keep count. I think there was a curiosity factor about me when I did the show on July 4th. I started by introducing myself more fully by telling my life story and the struggles through the orphanages and onto law school. I was comfortable doing the show and I wanted to do more!

I went home the next day. Ed was back in his chair and Holmey gave Ed a good report of my hosting. Ed listened to parts of the recorded show and they both agreed to give me another shot. That next shot came the following month and I went back to Fargo, this time spending time with Ed and Wendy. They invited me to stay at their house and we spent time relaxing and eating and chatting. They made me feel at ease; it was great. Their home is beautiful, situated on a lake in the woods, and they were *extremely* gracious hosts. They were the nicest people in the world!

The second show during that trip went very well too, and we started to discuss more guest host opportunities. I told them I would arrange for the ability to do the show from L.A. and make myself available to do the show anytime they needed it. Holmey said he would call the radio station there and see what they could do. But to be on the safe side,

I knew I needed to do something to give myself the ability to do the show from Los Angeles with something I could control.

In those days, Ed was on in Los Angeles on the progressive talk station KTLK, AM 1150. It's the same building where Stephanie Miller does her show and is literally three miles from where I live and work. Holmey was able to get that station to make their studios available to me, and I started doing shows from there. On November 15, 2006, I was hosting for Ed and our rescued basset hound, a girl named Elvis, was very sick. I had planned a joke for the show. The joke was, "My dog is sick, so I took her to the vet, and he took an x-ray. When we looked at the x-ray it was a slide show of the Bush Administration, so no wonder she was sick." But I really messed up the joke and that little voice in my head said, "Norm, that sounded awful, you had better explain or you'll sound like an idiot."

That show was a week after the Democrats had retaken Congress (both houses). The joke was delivered (or rather, mis-delivered) about halfway into the show. I brought my engineer Kozz with me to KTLK in Burbank, as he assisted me in doing the shows. He would be on the phone back to Fargo, and would feed me the calls and other show cues. The entire show on that day, to that point, had been taken up with people wanting to impeach Bush and imprison him for his war crimes in Iraq and lying us into that invasion. It was a very hot show—lots of emotion and debate. I was for not immediately impeaching. I wanted an investigation by Congress, lay out all the facts before the American people and *then* impeach the rat! Halfway in, I delivered the screwed-up joke.

When I began my explanation about Elvis, I started to cry—right on the air! I was choking up real bad and was a second away from simply breaking down on national radio.

I explained that Elvis was close to death and it was all very spontaneous. I was going to tell the joke and move on, but because I had screwed it up, I needed to explain and away it went. I managed to get control of myself, took a call from a guy in Seattle and struggled to the break. By that point, Kozz was crying, I was crying, it was very emotional.

Elvis knocked George W. Bush off the show for the rest of the day. During the last half of that show, I got calls and emails from everywhere, including the president of the Humane Society in Utah! Several listeners sent me "The Rainbow Bridge" which I reprint below. Have a hanky or tissues with you; take my word.

A few minutes after the show ended, I was on the phone back to Fargo doing our usual analysis and coaching. Holmey said, "Norm, Ed got off his plane about ten minutes before the show ended. He called me and asked, 'How's Norm doing? How's the show going?' and I told him you were on the air crying about your dog dying and he said, 'Wow, that's great radio, compelling radio. Everyone has a dog that died—that's great stuff!'" All I could think was, "Doesn't anyone care about my poor dog?" For the rest of that day and for days thereafter, I was deluged with email from people telling me about their dogs, their cats, their birds and iguanas and snakes and rabbits and horses and fish and all the other critters we have and fall in love with.

We did put Elvis to sleep on Sunday, November 18th, three days after the show. I was crying for days and am crying again now, writing this. Elvis was our second rescued basset. We had gotten her from a shelter. They said she was about eight years-old and we had her for five years. She had mange when we got her and was a mess. We've rescued several dogs and cats, including older, hard-to-place dogs, and one day I will write about them all. If you've spent time with me on the radio, you know we've talked about rescuing animals and that it's something near and dear to my heart.

The Rainbow Bridge

Just this side of heaven is a place called Rainbow Bridge.

When an animal dies that has been especially close to someone here, that pet goes to Rainbow Bridge.
There are meadows and hills for all of our special friends so they can run and play together.
There is plenty of food, water and sunshine, and our friends are warm and comfortable.

All the animals who had been ill and old are restored to health and vigor; those who were hurt or maimed are made whole and strong again, just as we remember them in our dreams of days and times gone by.
The animals are happy and content, except for one small thing; They each miss someone very special to them who had to be left behind.

They all run and play together, but the day comes when one suddenly stops and looks into the distance. His bright eyes are intent; His eager body quivers. Suddenly he begins to run from the group, flying over the green grass, his legs carrying him faster and faster.

You have been spotted, and when you and your special friend finally meet, you cling together in joyous reunion, never to be parted again. The happy kisses rain upon your face, your hands again caress the beloved head, and you look once more into the trusting eyes of your pet, so long gone from your life but never absent from your heart.

Then you cross Rainbow Bridge together. · · ·

—*Author unknown*

Around this time, the end of 2006, I realized that I should not rely on KTLK forever (ultimately, Ed *was* canceled off that station). I did some research and found that I could build an inexpensive basic "studio" in a spare room in my office. I bought some used equipment through eBay and borrowed equipment from the friends who had lent me their studio a few years earlier. They were thrilled to see my progression and were very happy to help. I set up a high-quality telephone line (an ISDN line) with AT&T so that I could do the show from Los Angeles without having to go through KTLK, and told Ed and Holmey I was ready to go on with a few minutes notice! I used that little studio dozens of times and it worked beautifully!

They kept calling me more and more to do the show when Ed was away. That holiday season, Christmas 2006, I did almost a weeks worth of shows and, with each one, my confidence grew and Ed, Holmey and the Fargo crew ("Team Fargo" as Ed calls them) got more comfortable with me doing it. I realized that I was now, informally, Ed's number one substitute and I was *absolutely* thrilled to the bone! Through it all, I kept wondering how my parents would feel (I suspect they would have been proud) and I constantly reminded myself that I had come a *very* long way from the rats, roaches and orphanages.

I started to arrange my law practice to leave Ed's slot (9 a.m. to noon, Pacific time) open in case I was needed for the show. Sometimes that was impossible, but I was almost always available to do Ed's show when Ed or Holmey called. And the show subbings kept piling up throughout 2007 and into 2008. In 2008, I started seriously considering launching our own show and consulted Ed and Holmey on it. They were both very encouraging and thought I could, and should, do it. I thought so, too! I started seriously winding down my law practice, not taking any new cases and resolving the ones I could. I figured that, at some point, there wouldn't be any left and I could declare my law career over! I even began making appearances with Ed. He did Town Halls in Tucson, Denver, Madison and a more informal gathering outside San Francisco, and he took me along on each one. The program director of the radio station in San Francisco, Green 960, said he had never seen a host bring his sub along. Based on the audience response, he was very happy Ed did! The audience seemed receptive so I was further encouraged that perhaps I *could* make a go of it.

Having done something like 30 shows for Ed by that time, I was totally hooked on talk radio. I had a series of conversations with Frances about making a career change and we decided to go for it. It would be a daunting task. I was approaching 50 and, although we had a nice amount of money saved up, launching a show with only us as owners was going to be expensive. Building a studio, hiring staff, paying for satellite time, all the incidentals of launching a talk radio show were going to require writing *a lot* of checks and there was no guarantee that anyone would pick up the show. We had decided to do this on our own—no investors, no backers, no one but us owning and controlling the show—and if it all worked, we'd be fine but if not, we'd have blown a gigantic sum of money.

With *all that* as background, there we were, Frances and I, at the end of 2008, early 2009. I was subbing for Ed regularly; I was disgusted with practicing law; and I was loving the talk radio we were doing. And despite the odds against us, we were deciding to launch our own show. Knowing that we had a certain amount of money to invest, and wary about the potential number of outlets on "traditional" radio stations, we began planning to launch *The Norman Goldman Show* at the end of 2009. We had a strategy to get on as many radio stations as we could, build an audience as best and as fast as we could, then use the Internet and other technologies (smart phone "apps" chief among them) to transition as many people as possible into our column (especially in areas where there were/are no radio stations carrying our type of program). That is the strategy we have implemented and it seems to be working. We have built a group of folks—and the numbers are growing—who like what we say and want to take back our country from the greed heads and charlatans who peddle themselves as the saviors of American purity.

* * * * *

12
THE SHOW TODAY

Since we launched the show in September 2009, we have been on about a dozen radio stations covering about 20 "rated markets," meaning we go into multiple Arbitron-rated areas on one radio station. For example, the San Francisco radio station KKGN covers the San Jose radio market, a separate Arbitron metropolitan area. Yet we're still not making money. Why? The advertising dollars are just not big enough to sustain our overhead. We'll keep working at it and hope to get to the breakeven point soon! That is why selling the podcasts of the show, doing the extra legal segments like "Beyond The Norm," and building up a group of direct financial supporters is so crucial. We no longer want to nor are we able to rely on fickle radio stations (which can toss us off at any time) and, frankly, the AM band is in trouble. People are listening to AM less and less, and some of these radio stations have less-than-excellent-signals, thereby diminishing the chance to reach a lot of people in that radio area. Though FM is slowly moving its talk stations to AM, I fear for the future of the AM band. Smart phones and "apps" seem to be the future combined with a group of people who pay $5 a month (or $50 a year, two months free) to keep us going.

As for the staff, we have Crysta, who is our producer. She books guests; handles the phone during the shows; works with me (and Mike) to get sound clips; finds story ideas; and helps with the computer record keeping we need to do. Mike is our associate producer; he uploads a lot of our content to the website; works with Crysta on the sound clips; works with me on the funny or silly sound clips that we use for comedic effect on the show; and also helps with creative ideas and stories. Kozz is our board operator/engineer who runs the show and programs the show computers. He also records and edits interviews and works with me as we do the actual live show. We use hand signals and a "talk back" intercom to communicate as the show progresses. Mark is our part-time support staffer who helps the other three staff members with their jobs and works with Mike to keep the show and "Beyond The Norm" segments uploaded for the people who subscribe. Frances is at home, listening to the show and going through the e-mails. She forwards me e-mails she thinks I should see and I am going through e-mails on air, too. Frances also catalogs the e-mails and, to the extent she can, tracks the number and locations they come from. We get email from all 50 states and countries all over the world. This is our team!

Our typical day involves me reading the paper (the *Los Angeles Times*, of course!) as we get going in the morning, looking on the Internet for stories, and suggesting interview subjects and topics to Crysta and Mike. For me, it is basically a 24/7 experience. I am always sending Crysta and Mike story ideas, interview suggestions and sound clip suggestions. I am also watching the corporate media/cable news channels for what *they* are talking about (I start watching these shows as soon as I open my eyes in the morning) and am posting things on Facebook and Twitter. I watch a variety of corporate media/cable news shows at night, after the show and before going to bed, and then the whole process starts all over again the next day!

We all gather in the studio in the mid-to-late morning and set about putting the show together. I am responsible for the "Beyond The Norm" segments that we do separately. I get ideas for that from lots of different places. I am always on the lookout for good "Beyond The Norm" segments. We record the BTN a couple of hours before the show and I post the topics to our website and Facebook about 30 minutes or so before the show. I spend a lot of time on Facebook: posting links, chatting with folks and generally getting involved with my fellow Facebookers. I know many people don't like Facebook (or Google, for that matter) due to their far-less-than-perfect-privacy policies, but for me, Facebook is a great way to interact with a lot of people at once.

On average we get 750 to 1,000 e-mails per week. I cannot answer them all, but I try to answer as many as I can. We get story suggestions, interview suggestions (and requests) and people arguing with me over what I have said on the air. We get lots of very nice e-mails and some very nasty ones, too. I enjoy them all!

With a staff of four and a half, we put on our show each and every day. I absolutely *love* every minute of it! The whole process is fun—the show preparation, working with the crew, the interactivity of the on-air calls and all the e-mails, being on Facebook and Twitter, watching the news all the time. Heck, *I always did that anyway* so the "being a news junkie" part is really no change from what I had always done, only now I just get to share my views and analysis with everyone!

Of all the elements of our show, the one that people respond to most is the "Senior Legal Analyst" part. Followed by a close second is the "Civics Class" thing we do, less as a discrete, separate element and more as simply a theme interwoven throughout the content. Since the first moment I went on the air with Ed, I have tried and always strive very hard to make the law *accessible and understandable*. Not only do we *all* pay for the law with our tax dollars (where do you think the courts get their operating budgets?), but so many people have so much interaction with the law all the time and it is so bewildering to them. I try to take the fear out of approaching the law and make the concepts and rulings make sense on a "typical person" level. Whether it is handling a car accident, a traffic stop and ticket, a lawsuit or end-of-life issues, the law is so important to all of us that I have put myself on a mission to de-mystify it and make it both interesting and comfortable for people.

One other thing I try to never forget about radio is it must be *entertaining*. People are usually listening in their cars (and in our time slot, on their way home from work) and others are doing housework or baking or gardening with the radio on while they work. Others are at their desks at the office. The common theme through all of this is that people want information, yes; the news up to the minute, of course; perspective on what is happening and analysis of events, certainly; but they also want to laugh and have a friend reaching out to them through the radio. For that reason, I do the dopey impersonations and play the silly sound clips (taken very deliberately out of context) to add spice to the show. I have collected a variety of things that people in the public eye have said (I owe huge thanks to Jim Healy, a late but not forgotten Los Angeles radio personality, who had hundreds of hilarious clips of which I have borrowed many), and intersperse them in the show. The beautiful thing about politicians is that they are public figures—anything they say in public is fair game and they *love* being recorded—so there is always new material around to be added to our ever-growing list of things that people say which can be added to the mix. It may be John Boehner saying, "Chicken crap" or "How about a glass of Merlot?" or Ronald Reagan saying, "Isn't that novel" or, of course, Bill Clinton's, "I did not have sexual relations with that woman. . . ." We play it all. Based on the response, it's a good element of the show!

✦ ✦ ✦ ✦ ✦

"Democrats never agree on anything, that's why they're Democrats. If they agreed with each other, they would be Republicans."   —Will Rogers

PART
3

POLITICS

13
THE VISION THING

So many of my friends on this, the correct side of the political divide, fail to recognize that the other side has *both* a long and short term strategy. I call it the "Pushing Strategy," just keep pushing in your direction and *never* stop. Don't let setbacks frustrate you. In fact, turn setbacks to your advantage. Spin events (there is *never* a setback; *everything* that happens is good), and never stop *pushing your agenda* in your direction. Push everyone and everything: *Always* call the media the "liberal media" even if they are the *extreme* opposite of liberal (there is never a "good enough" in the pushing strategy). Push the Tea Party to make the Republicon Party ever more insane; push the Democrats to always "moderate" their positions; push to cut and gut the social safety net; push extreme social issues and extreme ideology until homelessness is the fault of the homeless (their peril is due to their laziness). Turn "Christian" into "Calvinism," a sparse, go-it-alone-it's-all-your-fault-that-you're-in-this-mess-philosophy, and *never believe in boundaries. All things are possible, if you push hard enough.* We simply don't understand this about them. It's high time we did, and acted in response.

They adjust their *tactics* as conditions change, but the basic structures of the long and short term strategies do *not* change. The ultimate goal is to repeal the 20th Century. End Social Security (or better yet, *privatize* it so they can steal all the money), and do the same for Medicare (look at the Paul Ryan plan for Medicare—it's another giant corporate welfare program, transferring hundreds of billions of dollars of Medicare money to insurance companies). End child labor laws; end unions; end environmental protections; end regulations of food purity and water/air quality; end government support for the poor; end government hand-up programs like student loans; end public education.

It would have been laughable and politically unthinkable for Ronald Reagan or Gerald Ford to propose ending child labor laws. America was not yet *conditioned* for that level of extremism, but America is there now. The states are "experimenting" with ending child labor laws in Maine and Wisconsin. The states are "laboratories of democracy" indeed! They always have one or two candidates/politicians who are far off the deep end even for them, wherever they happen to be at any moment. This is part of the pushing strategy: Get people adjusted to where they are going while making the less insane people look moderate and rational. Michele Bachmann gives us a glimpse of their future; Ron Paul gives us a glimpse of their future; the other people (i.e., Newt Gingrich, Paul Ryan, Eric Cantor, Mitt Romney, and Chris Christie) are just not there yet, and look better compared to the edge-pushers.

They want to abolish the minimum wage and turn us all into dollar-a-day wage slaves. They say we must "compete" with the low wage countries while their corporate masters send our jobs *to* those low wage countries. We pay for it with our tax dollars through corporate welfare tax subsidies. They haven't gotten us pushed to abolish the minimum wage yet, but some of their "far out" candidates float it now to get us thinking about it while they move us toward that position some years down the road. This is how they operate: Move us step-by-step with one or a few people perceived to be "way out there," and make what was once unacceptable become acceptable—at least it's not crazy! Then what was once crazy becomes acceptable as a new crazy standard is articulated by their "fringe" leaders. They relentlessly push to get as far as they can go, and there is very little push back from the Democratic Party.

Their two most important goals: 1) End all taxes on the rich and big business, and 2) end regulations—*all* regulations—on big business. *Everything else* is either secondary or designed to trick people who are not rich into supporting their Party. That explains their views on abortion, religion and everything else. And they never lose sight of what I just told you. Part of their end regulation of big business agenda is to *destroy unions.* Have we seen any of *that* in the last 30 years?

By contrast, we have no strategy at all—not long term and not short term. *They* prioritize their list of issues beautifully— give the Devil his due—and we have no sense of importance. To us, *every single issue* is a blood feud between us. We battle each other to the death over *everything.* We treat each issue as of *equal importance*; we have no sense of proportion or priority. I attack President Obama over this or that program or decision and I get attacked viciously for *not attacking the President hard enough*! Simultaneously, I get attacked for attacking the President *at all*! There is no notion on our side of "chilling out" and keeping our perspective. There is *no discussion at all* as to what issues are our "most important/ core values." With agreement on *those*, we can disagree on the others of less importance. We are, as Will Rogers famously said in 1930, "members of no political organization—we are Democrats."

This is ironic considering we identify *them* as demanding ideological purity. The truth is the opposite. For almost four decades now, they have not gotten *Roe v. Wade* overturned; gays are getting married now; and support for same-sex marriage is growing. Individuals controlling their own end-of-life choices (think Dr. Kevorkian) and people supporting personal use of marijuana are supported by large numbers of people, but *they* don't care. Those issues mean nothing to them. They are only used as a means to an end, which is to get their sheep, pardon me, voters to support their twin big (and only) goals: End all taxes on the rich and end all regulations on big business.

Time and time again, their sheep have been used, manipulated and disappointed by their "leaders" who use these social wedge issues to gin up their energy, then cast them aside when the money issues inevitably dominate their Party. Yet that does not stop their ground troops from believing and forgiving and fighting some more. Their leaders recognize and understand this, their Lucys always know that when they put that football down, their legions of Charlie Browns will line up to try to kick the ball every time. When their sheep got angry *at* big business—in the initial "Tea Party" days of 2007—that anger was quickly turned into Koch brother-run hatred of *government regulation of* big business. Their "leaders" know how to control their troops. Ignore the fact that the Tea Party began with anger *at* big business and quickly became support *for* big business and a raging demand for more of the same criminality that caused the Tea Party in the first place. Their sheep have no sense of irony; indeed, their sheep are easily manipulated.

On our side, we are the ones demanding ideological purity on all issues at all times. We ridicule *them* for it, but the truth is they submerge their differences on many issues for their two key goals. We tear each other limb from limb on *every* issue, regardless of whether that issue is linked to our core values.

And *that* is really the issue: What *are* our core values? They know theirs—no taxes on the rich and no regulation of big business. Simple, elegant and extreme. Our list is endless. We object to (and properly so) virtually everything our leaders do, very rarely giving a pass on anything. I've been guilty of this myself, perhaps more so than most. I offer these thoughts not to scold you or us, but rather to help us see the big picture and then work to figure out our strategies.

We need a long and short term vision. We cannot treat each event, each disappointment, and each debate as if it were the end of the world. And we *do*. With regard to President Obama, many of us are sorely disappointed in his weakness, accommodations and sell-outs. Yet for the short term, I will support him, if only to keep the presidency away from the lunatics on their side, and to hope for a Supreme Court vacancy or two or three which will be filled by non-insane people. This is, admittedly, a lowered-expectations strategy. It is a short term plan—*very* short term. This is acceptable if we settle upon a longer term strategy.

On the bright side, we did scratch a really big item off our to do list. We elected a guy named Barack Hussein Obama as President, looking the way he looks, with that name, so few years after the white Protestant elite declared holy war on Muslims. Next up, the first woman President! Let's acknowledge our victories where we can and concentrate on our own "Pushing Strategy."

Do you think the Koch brothers, Richard Mellon Scaife, Philip Anschutz, Richard DeVos and all the greedheads on their side just woke up one morning and, like magic, the United States was theirs for the reshaping? They have worked, relentlessly and with a long term strategy, to get to where they have dragged us today. And they have adjusted their strategies as time and events have warranted. They did not want President Obama. But they *used him* to further their goals—"socialism" was on the march! Call the troops to the front! America is being taken away from you by the blacks! A Muslim, fascist, socialist, elitist agenda of abortion-on-demand-terrorist-appeasing-America-hating-liberals had taken over! Call the troops to the front! It's a government takeover! What we need is even less regulation of big business and even fewer taxes on the rich!

The Koch brothers (and their daddy, Fred, who was even crazier than his two boys) were so radical, so extreme, that in the 1960s, they were denounced and shunned by the Republican Party led, amazingly, by William F. Buckley and his corporate elitist cronies, who claimed the Republican Party for their own. Recall that the Koch daddy was one of the founders of the John Birch Society, a rabidly anti-Communist, conspiracy-theory-loving racist group that would remind any fair-minded person of fascism. However, the Kochs did not give up when they were ousted from the Replublicon Party, they plotted and planned and worked to take over. They didn't, like us, rend their clothes, declare the world had ended and cry themselves to sleep in a bath of self pity. They redoubled their efforts, gritted their teeth, developed a long term strategy and *got to work*!

First, the Koch boys looked at a long-term horizon. They reconciled themselves to not achieving their goals for years or even decades. They settled in for a long war, linking every day's actions to their long term goals. And what are those two long term goals? Have you forgotten *already*? They then set about defining just what long-term "success" was, and settled on their long-term agenda. "Success" was the end of taxes on themselves and their rich brethren; the end of regulations on themselves and their giant corporate brethren; and the subjugation of the American people to a low-wage, long-hours work life that resembled America in the 1800s.

The Kochs looked lovingly back at America in the *laissez faire* period before the rise of Franklin Roosevelt, and decided that America had to return to those golden days. Antitrust laws? To make companies stay *not* huge? Make them unenforced. National labor standards? Neutralize the regulator or get "enforcement" sent to the states, where they could be unenforced. (It's a states' rights matter, don't you see?) Destroy unions by any means necessary—public unions, private unions, *destroy all unions*. Also, send the jobs overseas where these pesky workers' rights issues and environmental regulations don't exist. This stripping of the federal government's power to help the 99% is Ron Paul's argument and that of the Koch brothers: "Enforce the Constitution." In their view, keep the federal government limited to its core role: endless spending on endless war, nothing more, and let Halliburton profit from the endless war since we're there anyway. All these issue positions *feed back to the two goals that define who they are*. Do you remember their two goals? Look at their *policies*—either those policies feed back to accomplish their two goals or they are designed to trick the sheep to keep supporting the Party which will work to achieve the two goals. When you analyze the Koch brother Republicons this way, it makes perfect sense. You and I are like Perry Mason: *We* are figuring out *their* scheme; *they* have known it all along.

They also use *fear* and *fear of the foreigner* to manipulate. This is old stuff, but newly adapted. The old war against "the communists" is now the new war against "the terrorists." It is the same playbook—"There's a communist under every bed" became "There's a terrorist under every bed." The old "Democrats are soft on communism" became "Democrats are soft on terrorism." Telling people that hordes of illegal brown-skinned people (pardon me, *Mexicans*) are coming here to take our jobs and destroy our culture is a classic old trick. It was done with the Irish, the Italians, the Jews, the Chinese, every group that has come to these shores has had that nasty trick perpetrated upon them. We saw it recently with President Obama. He's a Muslim, don't you know? Born in Kenya, don't you know? He's not one of *us*, he's the other, the foreigner, here to destroy *our* pure culture and heritage. This use of fear is very effective. It worked with the communists and now it works with the terrorists. It justifies whopping war budgets and global military domination (more money to steal for corporate welfare) while hiding the theft behind fear and patriotism.

How to accomplish the two goals was the Koch question. Remember, they were on the outs with their political party. They were considered pariahs and extremists by their own supposed friends. So what to do to re-take what they believed was rightfully their country?

They refined their ideology. Funding the fear machine is always a good bet. Having Al Qaeda and the September 11, 2001 attacks to scare people is a good device. Keeping their goals of no taxes on the rich and no regulation of big business ever uppermost in their minds, they jettisoned the *overt* racism of the Birchers, turning to *covert* racism, with code words like "welfare queens," "freeloaders" and "Muslim terrorists." They realized they could create a coalition—an odd one but a winning one nevertheless—by melding racists, religionists and the rich into one group. They could get the social warriors/religionists on their side with issues like the permissiveness of the new social mores of the 1960s (these long-haired hippie freaks with their marijuana and free love; why, heck you can't tell the boys from the girls!) and in this way, Roe v. Wade (1973) was a *huge* gift to them, a gift that keeps on giving. They *cannot* have Roe v. Wade overturned, that would take the power out of their use of the issue.

Do you see how they stay flexible, incorporate and adapt events and conditions to relentlessly march forward to their goals? Whenever *anything* happens, the Kochs and their purchased brains, i.e., Karl Rove, Roger Ailes and Frank Luntz, immediately think, "How can we spin this to return to pushing our twin goals?" Because the racists and religious extremists don't care about taxes or regulation but they do care about the "decline of American morals," the Kochs realized that they could be moved into the Koch column. They created and used easy to remember sound bites like "government handouts," "welfare queens," "the homosexual agenda" and "food stamps" to signal that the decline of American morals was caused by blacks and gays and Democrats feeding the lazy good-for-nothings with *your* tax dollars. Their intended audiences heard them loud and clear. What was once an acceptable appeal to obvious racism had to go covert, and it did. This is now called "dog whistle politics" in the corporate media. The Kochs realized that the groups inside this new Republicon coalition did not compete with each other, rather, they complemented each other since big business couldn't care less about black people, gays and abortion. They cared only about no taxes on the rich and no regulation of big business.

Having folded the racists and religious crazies into their group, the Kochs needed to find a way to justify the end of regulation of big business that made it sound good and patriotic to go along with the destruction of government. This was easy. They knew there was a strong DNA strand of skepticism and fear of government power that traced all the way back to the nation's very founding. After all, we became the United States to throw off the heavy yoke of a distant and powerful king who taxed us without representation. They took the themes of "freedom and liberty" and twisted them into "being free of government regulation of business" instead of *individual liberty against a big, overbearing government.* If the true meaning of freedom and liberty were promoted or understood, women would have a right to choose and gays could marry the mate of their choice. By counting on the intellectual vapidity of their followers to not question why they were simultaneously demanding small government when it came to protecting us all from predatory business practices yet demanding hugely intrusive government when it came to interfering in the intimate life choices of average citizens, the Kochs built their coalition. And it's worked—their followers have never questioned or apparently realized the utter contradiction of the slogans and mantras they chant. As Forrest Gump would say, "Stupid is as stupid does."

The Koch boys had one more massive advantage—money. Money can buy a lot of things, especially people to do your bidding. Buying brains to concoct slogans and plans is easy when you have such vast sums to tap and throw around. Getting these themes developed, with the accompanying slogans like "Government doesn't create jobs, business creates jobs" and

"Lower taxes on the job creators" or "Job killing tax hikes" along with "Liberal social engineering" and "Government picking winners and losers," gives the gloss of ideology to their goals, and that gloss of ideology springs from deep strains of anti-government American thought.

George Lakoff, professor of linguistics at the University of California at Berkeley, has been sounding this alarm for a very long time. His theory (with which I heartily agree) of "framing" is a brilliant analysis of how the Kochs and their minions evoke a whole tidal wave of vague but deeply embedded popular ideas and emotions by triggering these ideas and emotions with just a few words. This type of mind manipulation is amazingly effective (give the Devil his due again) especially when practiced on those with superficial grounding in politics, history and current events. In short, it's easy to manipulate idiots.

* * * * *

14
THEIR VISION IMPLEMENTED
ECONOMIC ANARCHY

For the Koch brothers was born a working strategy for a new governing coalition merging racism, religious zealotry, anti-government beliefs and trust in business primacy. The next tasks were how to conquer the Republicon Party and implement their vision. For this, they also settled in for the long fight. They seeded "think tanks" and incubated "intellectuals" who created theories, policy papers and the aforementioned snappy and memorable sound bites to further their cause. But, and this part is crucial, they were *patient—not impatient*. They understood their plan could and likely *would* take decades to advance. *Our impatience*, by contrast, leads us to many problems— self-inflicted wounds—while we tear ourselves to shreds over not having instant success, which is perhaps a byproduct of the modern age of instant gratification and instant results for everything. We fail to even formulate a long term plan or vision. We don't have an idea or vision for what "success" is in 10, 20 or 30 years.

The Kochs have created or sponsored the Cato Institute, Americans for Prosperity, American Enterprise Institute,

Heritage Foundation, Freedom Works, Federalist Society, Washington Legal Foundation, Manhattan Institute, Americans for Tax Reform, National Taxpayers Union, and the Reason Foundation. And this is only a *partial* list. It also includes the Ann Coulters and Michelle Malkins of the chattering and book-writing classes; the Limbaughs, Levins and Hannitys of talk radio; Fox News Channel (which I call Fox Boobs, since that word works on several levels); and the constant demands that "media" simply report whatever wacky statements these people make. On pain of being accused of "a liberal bias", i.e., "the liberal media," all work together to blanket the American airwaves and American minds with propaganda, their propaganda. What media they cannot buy, they intimidate. And it works. Just look around you.

They have bought up radio stations and other media. The owners of radio stations are decidedly aligned with the Republicon Party. There are huge swaths of America (think the South and Midwest) where there are three or four radio stations constantly pounding the message of the Kochs into the minds of listeners delivered by their tools, the "Limbecks." I call them the Limbecks because they are all one mouth, there are just a whole lot of them. Whether Jerry Doyle and Rusty Humphries, Hugh Hewitt and Dennis Prager, Laura Ingraham and Mark Levin, Michael Savage (real name—Weiner) and Sean Hannity, Rush Limbaugh and Glenn Beck, they have a huge number of national hosts who can stock three or four radio stations in one city after another. They also have a deep bench of local corporate tools who aspire to Limbaugh-dom and constantly play "loony leap-frog" to see who can say the most outrageous thing. If all you ever hear is one side of an argument, you will believe it, especially when it is so smoothly and scientifically formulated and delivered to propagandize for maximum effect. Fox Boobs of course is the king of the corporate propaganda television machine, but the other broadcast networks also play to the crazies, competing for audience. Just as a pace car in racing gets the field of race cars moving, Fox Boobs and the radio dominance sets the pace for the other media to follow along. After a slow start on using the Internet as an organizing device, the corporatists have also adapted to this new communication medium to get their word out: *World Net Daily*, *News Max* and the *Drudge Report* get huge numbers of hits from the crazies looking for "birther" stories and other fantasies to feed their paranoid delusional minds. And the Kochs delight in it all; the fools to be used for their twin goal agenda. Just to review, what are those two goals again?

The traditional networks, seeing their market share constantly eroded by the proliferation of cable and other entertainment choices, desperately try to maintain their highest possible audience, to get the highest possible advertising dollar. Not wanting to offend anyone, and feeling the heat of the Koch brothers-fueled campaign branding them "the liberal media," these broadcast outlets pander to the fringe extremists, giving an equivalency to their crazy views (just look at the "Obama-was-not-born-here" stupidity) and thus elevate what were heretofore fringe views into legitimacy by placing them side-by-side with actually rational and true facts. Climate change is a marvelous example. The world scientific community is virtually unanimous, and virtually all the research proves that human activity has dramatically altered the world environment. Melting of the polar caps, ever-increasing extreme weather events, Greenland and polar ice shelves literally breaking apart indicate there is mounting daily evidence that our activities have altered the climate. Yet the Koch brothers (who are major oil and gas people) have a vested interest in denying this and keeping us all addicted to the heroin of oil with the gas pump being the equivalent of the addict's needle. They fund their mouthpieces (who are, of course, glad to take the money) to propagate the notion that climate change is a hoax, and because they have bullied the corporate media (that's you I'm talking about CBS, NBC, ABC and CNN) into providing their "side" as equally legitimate, this false view is now peddled as equally valid and legitimate to a deliberately confused public.

The television viewer and radio listener is now implicitly told that "journalism" means simply presenting two arguments, side by side, with no examination of the merits of each argument. The corporate media thus satisfies itself that it is doing journalism by being "fair and balanced" and giving both sides equal weight and time, despite the fact that one side is demonstrably false. Telling us that "There are those who contend the Earth rotates around the Sun, but others claim the Earth is the center of the universe and the Sun rotates around the Earth" is not journalism. It is parroting the statements of two sides, without any effort to provide an *answer* that comports with *facts and science.*

Another sadly excellent example is evolution. Poor Mr. Darwin has been under attack from the moment he published *On the Origin of Species* in 1859. Yet his work has been proven scientifically correct over and over again. We see examples proving his point in our own lives—antibiotics wipe out a strain of bacteria or disease only to be replaced by a "superbug" that evolved to evade the vaccine or medicine and take the place of its wiped out predecessor. Simple study of history shows how certain dinosaur birds evolved into the birds we have today, and so forth. Yet the extremists demand that the media give their baseless assertions of "God" and "the Bible" equal time on pain of being accused of being "the liberal media." The corporate media (which is not liberal) obligingly goes along. Even worse, these extremists have taken over school boards (been to Texas lately?) and re-write the science books to discredit the science of evolution and substitute "creationism" in its place. It got so bad that Lynne Cheney (wife of former illegal, illegitimate Vice President Dick Cheney) wanted to re-write school books to take out all the examples of the United States government doing bad things such as all the bad things we have done to Native Americans. Trail of Tears, anyone?

* * * * *

15

"SMALL GOVERNMENT"= ECONOMIC ANARCHY

In the last 30 years, we have seen America relentlessly *pushed* to the corporate side. The ideological support structure for this is the Koch brothers and their friends' financial wealth, creating dozens of "think tanks" and funding numerous people and spouts for their philosophy across all platforms—print, television, radio and the Internet. Their leaders exemplify this march to greed. Willard "Mitt" Romney headed a business (founded in 1984) called Bain Capital. He and his partners bought companies such as Domino's Pizza, Burlington Coat Factory, Guitar Center, Hospital Corporation of America, Clear Channel Radio (yes, Mitt Romney was involved with the radio industry that puts Limbaugh and company on the air; he has since left the company) and others. Relentlessly focused on cost cutting, Bain Capital fires employees, slashes budgets and squeezes the money out of the companies. This very employee-unfriendly company has yielded Romney a $250 million fortune on the backs of workers. In the 1980s, when Mitt Romney was founding Bain Capital, there was a person used called a "corporate raider" who would invest in companies, then demand big cuts, "maximizing value" (a nice term, don't you think?) through downsizing or liquidating and always waging war on the workers. This became so prevalent that many publicly traded companies enacted defenses to these tactics, called "poison pills," and other techniques to stop the pirate raiders from stealing or looting the companies. Notice that the 1980s coincided with Ronald Reagan's presidency. Ivan Boesky was a Wall Street stock trader who orchestrated an insider trading scheme which netted him a huge fortune—and prison time. Michael Milken created the "junk bond" market at this same time and netted himself a fortune—and prison time.

In the late 1980s the savings and loan banks collapsed. They did this because Ronald Reagan fostered laws and a culture that transformed these quiet little banks, which had served the valuable role of financing home loans for families, into pirate banks with risk-taking investors that gambled with government-insured money. Does *this* sound familiar? A total of $88 billion dollars was lost when 747 savings and loans failed. Before Reagan, failure was virtually unheard of; government regulation prevented such things from happening. Under Reagan, the savings and loans were deregulated—does *this* sound familiar?

At this time, one of the S&Ls was Silverado Savings of Colorado. A young man named Neil Bush (George W.'s brother and George H.W.'s son) was on the board of directors. The bank's collapse cost taxpayers 1.3 billion dollars. A government investigation after the collapse found Neil Bush had breached fiduciary duties and engaged in various conflicts of interest. No criminal charges were ever brought, but a civil lawsuit resulted in Neil paying $50,000.00—that's right, $50,000.00—and a fundraiser was set up by the Republicon establishment to help him pay *that*. A later divorce proceeding involving Neil and his ex-wife brought out admissions (in a deposition, under oath) of sex with prostitutes. Family values indeed! In 2003, evidence was brought forth showing Neil was paid millions in stock by Grace Semiconductor, a business with which Neil had no knowledge. Could it be because his brother was in the White House?

Sarah Palin was shown, through the release of e-mails in 2011, to be focused on becoming John McCain's running mate in 2008. She and her team went on a quiet lobbying effort to get McCain to pick her. Once they lost, she quickly lost interest in being governor of Alaska and quit, returning to the lower 48 seeking additional fame, and a whole lot of fortune. Millions of dollars later, Palin is still fleecing her flock for big cash. If you are willing to do the Koch brothers' bidding— to further the twin goals of the corporate agenda—you can become very rich. Of course, the fact that you are destroying America and your fellow Americans never seems to be part of the discussion.

In 1987 a movie called *Wall Street* was a big hit. Michael Douglas portrayed Gordon Gecko, a high-flying Wall Street type who delivered the famous line: "Greed, for lack of a better word, is good." This was during the Reagan Administration—a time during which Nancy Reagan, the First Lady, was clad in expensive furs, sumptuous diamonds and jewelry and the rich folks were engaged in conspicuous consumption. This same style recurred in the years of George W. Bush, when vast fortunes were amassed by a small group of wealthy Wall Street and corporate chieftains, many of whom paid little in taxes due to favorable laws purchased at their behest from Congress. Of course, when it all came crashing down in 2008, we the taxpayers were obligingly there to pick up the pieces, powder their little bottoms, give them soothing words and love pecks on the foreheads and take on to *our backs* the losses of their predatory ways.

Now, a scant three years later, the good times are rolling once again (this time under a Democratic President who has refused to take them on) with record corporate profits while unemployment, income inequality and the wealth divide are at historic highs. In short, the rich are richer, the poor poorer, and the middle class is sliding back into the poverty from which they once climbed out with a government hand up, not a hand out. Whether it was the G.I. Bill, social insurance programs such as Social Security, Medicare, Workers Compensation Insurance, Unemployment Insurance or fairness to unions, government action helped create a large and thriving middle class. With government under attack since the 1980s, these programs (and unions) are disappearing, and the progress made because of their existence is vanishing as well.

Antitrust laws have been on the books in America since the Sherman Antitrust Act of 1890. These laws were enacted because corporate pirates were concentrating vast amounts of money and power in a few hands and abusing consumers. Whether it was the Rockefeller oil monopoly (does *that* name sound familiar?) under the Standard Oil brand or the "robber barons" of finance (Jay Gould) or the Carnegie steel trust (does *that* name sound familiar?) or any number of others, like the railroads, capitalism was being perverted by a massive concentration of wealth and power that warped competition and harmed consumers. Government was seen as a force to prevent and check these private powers. Government, to use an analogy taken from nature, was the natural predator to help keep the natural balance of things in order. What happens when, in any natural environment, one of the predators is taken out leaving the environment to the other participants? If frogs are wiped out from a pond, what happens to the insect population? The answer is obvious—an imbalance occurs, and without any natural predators to keep the other species in check, one or more species gets out of control. Such is the case here when government is taken out of the role of natural predator for corporate greed and growth. We accept checks and balances in nature; we accept this in government (Congress checks the President, the Supreme Court checks Congress and so on), but when it comes to big business we are told to just let the predators do whatever they want and all will be good.

When they say they love "small government" they do *not*. They love economic anarchy. Their *social issues agenda is huge government*. Overbearing, intrusive and authoritarian. Think abortion, marijuana use, police surveillance of people with GPS tracking units secretly placed in the underside of cars (with no warrant, no judge's order, no nothing other than the police wanting to track us), end-of-life decisions (poor Terri Schiavo in Florida) and marriage equality. The "war on terror" is an open invitation to *massive government* in many areas. They *love* big government—just not on economic issues. On economic issues, it's economic anarchy. The Koch brothers and their cohorts have convinced their sheep that *only* in the realm of regulating big business, must there be "small government." Look at where this economic anarchy has gotten us in the last 30 years.

* * * * *

16

WE ONCE KNEW BETTER
THAN THIS NONSENSE

Between 1933 and the Reagan years, government regulation kept America from having deep recessions and wild swings—going from bubble to bust, a cycle that permeated America prior to the Great Depression and has returned since Reagan. The highs were steady and smooth, and the lows were milder than what we have seen lately. The highs and lows were smoothed out—the highs were lower and the lows were higher—and big growth occurred in the *middle class* and the national wealth. Before the Great Depression, America had what were then known as "Panics." We had a big one in 1907 (leading to the Federal Reserve System of 1913) and periodically throughout American history (1816, 1825, 1837, 1857, 1873, 1893) usually because of speculative bubbles and wild economic risk taking. This boom and bust cycle was generally accepted as the natural order of a capitalist system: banks failed, savings were wiped out, jobs vanished. Sound familiar? As America grew, the busts got bigger and deeper. The nation was especially freaked out by the Panic of 1907. By the time of the Great Depression (which was actually the

Panic of 1929), America had grown to the point where the bust caused such widespread havoc that government intervention was demanded in the election of 1932. From that time on, until 1980, government regulation of the markets kept the boom and bust cycle significantly in check. Antitrust laws were enforced and businesses were kept from being "too big to fail."

As an example, in 1966 the U.S. Supreme Court prevented the merger of two supermarket chains in Southern California. The Court prevented Von's Grocery Company from acquiring Shopping Bag Food Stores. There are some very notable and instructive aspects to this case. The merger occurred in 1960 when Dwight Eisenhower was president, a Republican. *A Republican administration sued to stop a merger!* Also, shortly before the merger, Von's was third in market share; Shopping Bag Foods was sixth. At the time of the merger in 1960, their sales *combined* were a mere 7.5 % of the market. And there is this, taken directly from the Court's decision:

> *From 1948 to 1958 the number of Von's stores in the Los Angeles area practically doubled from 14 to 27, while at the same time the number of Shopping Bag's stores jumped from 15 to 34. During that same decade, Von's sales increased fourfold and its share of the market almost doubled while Shopping Bag's sales multiplied seven times and its share of the market tripled....[T]he number of owners operating single stores in the Los Angeles retail grocery market decreased from 5,365 in 1950 to 3,818 in 1961. By 1963, three years after the merger, the number of single-store owners had dropped still further to 3,590. [Footnote omitted] During roughly the same period, from 1953 to 1962, the number of*

chains with two or more grocery stores increased from 96 to 150. While the grocery business was being concentrated into the hands of fewer and fewer owners, the small companies were continually being absorbed by the larger firms through mergers. [United States v. Von's Grocery Co., 1966, 384 U.S. 270]

The Supreme Court, at the behest of a Republican president, stopped a merger because a supermarket would have 7.5% of the market in a large geographic area! Also note that owners of two or more stores numbered 150; presently, there are far less than a dozen. Today in Southern California, one chain (Ralph's) easily has more than one-third of the market share, and in some areas, *almost all* of the market. My, how times have changed! This also shows America was a real capitalist country in those days—as recently as 1960! A large group of competitors, of modest or small size, with relatively low barriers to entry into that market, and a government (aligned with a court system) that kept a watchful eye on the competitive balance of the marketplace. Note that the Supreme Court saw growth of the two chains—growth was not "bad,"in fact, it was perfectly legitimate. What was *not* legitimate was growing *so large* that monopolistic power could be exercised with harm to competition and consumers. Those very same laws are on the books today. They are simply not enforced, not by Democratic nor Republicon administrations.

We have returned to the days before 1933. We have regressed to the days of wild booms and busts. We have recreated the robber baron days of the late 1800s and early 1900s where a few giant companies dominated markets and abused the public. We are witnessing an era when politicians of both parties are so weak, so corrupt, so hobbled and compromised that the days of yesteryear have returned—with the same disastrous consequences. We are back to the past! Let's party like it's 1929!

The culprit for much of this regression is the atmosphere that has been fostered in America since the ascension of Ronald Reagan in 1980. The belief that "greed is good," that rules should not exist or won't be enforced even if they do exist, has caused us to return to the bad old days before 1933. Except now, we have federal government-sponsored *socialism*—capitalistic socialism—if you will allow me the term. Today, ten banks control 77% of the assets on deposit. These banks are larger now than they were when the New Great Depression began with the crash in September 2008. These banks remain federally insured. They are officially declared "too big to fail" yet the banks are still holding a lot of power and money with insufficient government oversight.

In 1999 President Clinton signed the Gramm-Leach-Bliley law, which repealed the Glass-Steagall Act of 1933 and knocked down the wall separating speculation by "investment" banks with "depository" banks that were managed much more conservatively and with robust government oversight plus FDIC insurance. Glass-Steagall (officially the Banking Act of 1933) established the Federal Deposit Insurance Corporation (FDIC) and erected the wall, reasoning that if banks have their deposits insured against loss, they could not take risks with that money, at least not without a lot of eyes looking over their shoulders and telling them, "No, you cannot do that." By knocking down that wall, yet leaving the insurance in place, banks were now free to use their whopping amounts of deposits to make risky investments and pay themselves vast bonuses. The government (under George W. Bush) stood intentionally idly by, thinking the "magic of the marketplace" would cure all ills. Of course, the same wild speculation and bubble mentality that had occurred during all the "Panics" of the 1800s and early 1900s recurred, and this time we had a New Great Depression. Further, the abuse of housing mortgages—the placement of virtually anyone into a home with a mortgage that they could not afford, and then packaging those mortgages into "securities" (and getting the "rating agencies" to bless them with AAA ratings—a scandal no one has yet been held accountable for) and selling them to unsuspecting buyers (and lying about the quality, or lack of quality, of those mortgages), created a speculative and feeding frenzy bubble, allowing banks and the greed heads to gorge on fees and sales while creating the conditions for the crash of epic proportions in which we are still mired.

* * * * *

17

THE KOCH BROTHERS
TRIUMPH BEYOND THEIR
WILDEST DREAMS

At the heart of this all is an "every man for himself" *philosophy*. The *ideology* of "I got mine, you go get yours and if you don't, it's your tough luck, blame yourself" has turned America into a rigged game where insiders make the rules and steal the loot, and everyone else is fleeced. While we saw this with the savings and loan scandal of the late 1980s, it really hit big with George W. Bush and the fraud of the Wall Street gang in the decade of the 2000s. George W. Bush and the Wall Street crowd (plus their feeders, the mortgage brokers and bankers who sold these mortgages, funneling them to the Wall Street bankers while, of course, taking their cuts before passing on the loans) recreated the conditions of the 1920s, leading a wild speculative bubble, and then the inevitable bust.

Except this time, something else big changed. The government (again, George W. Bush) came rushing in with *bailouts*; bailed out by our federal government-sponsored socialism, also known as capitalistic socialism, where the good times are capitalist and the bad times are socialist—socialism for the rich and big business. The rule now is to *privatize the gains* and *socialize the losses*. When times are good, when the bubble is inflating, the captains of industry gorge themselves on the good times and extol the virtues of capitalism. Then when the bubble bursts and the crash happens, these same captains of commerce come crawling to the federal government crying, "Bail us out, please help us," and the federal government, gorged itself on a tiny sliver of the money from the good times (called campaign contributions; I call them bribes) obliges, and the taxpayers are fleeced. Privatize the gains, socialize the losses. By socialize is meant "spread through the society," meaning the taxpayers are on the hook.

* * * * *

18

THE KOCHS WORKED
FROM A DEEP VEIN OF
AMERICAN THOUGHT

The Kochs could not have succeeded without tapping into a deep vein of the American experience. What they have done is take a *My Weekly Reader* version of Adam Smith's *Wealth of Nations*, combined it with the vicious narcissism of Ayn Rand's twisted theory of "It's all about whatever I want to make me feel good," and then merged all of *that* fanatical craziness with a Puritanical, Calvinist-style of Lutheranism that turns the teachings of Jesus upside down. Their twisted and patently false version of Jesus is that the poor, the disabled, and the meek are that way *because it's their own fault* and God wants them that way. That's the Calvinism part. Therefore, no one need do anything to help them and in fact it is *better* to kick them when they're down because *the winners have been chosen by God because they are special and the little people are not*. This is why the 'Cons say, "Government shouldn't pick winners and losers (because God does)," although they do indeed pick winners and losers with their federal budget corporate welfare ways.

For their sheep, it's about what they *say*, not what they *do*. They then claim that *one thousand, five hundred years after*

Jesus, these harsh, Calvinist, screw-you religious dogmas are *the actual teachings of Jesus*, and they claim to be on a divine mission from God to impose this mental illness on the rest of us. This quadruple header of bizarre religious twistedness, stupidity, economic anarchy/*laissez-faire* corporate, crony, criminal capitalist greedy fanaticism *and* evangelism is the religious and theoretical underpinning of today's Republicon Party. But it all came from *somewhere*—not thin air.

It started with Martin Luther rejecting the Roman Catholic Church and it's debasement into materialism in the Middle Ages. This led to his excommunication from the Church around 1520. John Calvin then came along (1530s) and added a harshness with the concept of predetermination as decreed by God: *You are who you are because God chose that path for you, and there is nothing you can do about it*. This was taken a step further by the English Puritans, who additionally refined it when coming to America in the 1600s, with their Martin Luther/Calvinist-inspired Protestant work ethic, self-denial and asceticism. Remember, God has decreed we are all sinners, all we can do to win a place in Heaven is work hard, deny ourselves pleasures and live a chaste, spare life. Combine this with fanaticism and evangelism (the early Puritans in America persecuted and killed Quakers and burned witches at the stake), and then *layer on top of this religion* a very dumbed-down version of Adam Smith's *capitalism*, which has nothing to do with religion. Add to all *that* the Ayn Rand, "I should be free to do anything and everything I want, with no restrictions at all," and you have an ideology that demands the accumulation of wealth through hard work with the use of that wealth for God's work (evangelism) and the imposition of this view on all others (the Puritans of the Massachusetts Bay Colony were bigoted, intolerant and messianic) thus leading us to, and explaining,

John D. Rockefeller and Sarah Palin! Never underestimate the power of fanaticism, evangelism and religious dogma—just ask Osama bin Laden, Pat Robertson and Jerry Falwell. Somewhere along the way, the chaste and spare life parts got left behind—greed is good, according to capitalism!

According to Adam Smith and others, capitalism is defined as an economic system that in theory requires, among other conditions, many competitors of roughly equal size, full and complete information to consumers, and low or no barriers to entry into markets for new competitors—unlike the Rockefeller concentration of vast markets in one set of hands. John D. Rockefeller, the world's first billionaire, created a vast fortune via *a warped version of capitalism* with sharp and illegal business practices. Nevertheless, he gave away dimes and nickels asking what people would do with them. The source of this "Waste not, want not" philosophy was his *religion*, a religion based (in his case, Baptist) upon the Puritan and Protestant work ethic he inherited from his European ancestors. Despite having a fortune *so* massive he could literally light cigars with 100 dollar bills (although, due to his religion, he totally abstained from both alcohol and tobacco), every nickel and dime was precious and not to be spent frivolously. This is the chaste and spare lifestyle part. This merger of economic theory with religious theory has been taken to its logical extreme by many Americans without even understanding the historical antecedents that got them there.

Of course, being human, the religiously motivated self-denial, self-discipline, abstinence and asceticism all gave way to self-indulgence. The economically motivated accumulation of wealth became the glorification of objects and "greed is good" philosophy. Physicality led to the inevitable engagement in sexual escapades and yet, Puritan evangelism (later seeded into most Protestant denominations and Catholicism in America) and the demand to impose one's views on all others, remains. Since many others also want to control the world and all its people (Osama bin Laden anyone?), we in America have our own combination of old time religion, modern gluttony and aggressive evangelism with our evangelism being about religion, capitalism and democracy.

The hard work element of the Protestant work ethic remains in America as a very good basis for capitalism, and a very good way to attack unions and the enrichment of labor. But the social/cultural side of self-denial, plain living and chastity has been abandoned except as a weapon to attack others. The hypocrisy that this leads to brings us to our current situation with evangelicals such as Pastor Jimmy Swaggart, found with a prostitute; former Senator Larry Craig claiming he is *not* gay and yet trolling for gay sex in a Minneapolis airport men's room; and current Louisiana Senator David Vitter, proclaiming family values *while* visiting prostitutes. The other examples are far too numerous to mention. "Evangelical Christians" violating their own principles could fill a separate book.

Since America was founded on dislike for government trampling on *personal liberties*, the Kochs have twisted that into trampling on *big business*, added the religious ancestry of Calvinism and tapped into (and manipulated) the American mind. Of course, warping the suspicion of "big government" into a claim that *big business should not be regulated* is simply part of the 'Con job. We must return to the true meaning of "limited government" by refocusing it on the *protection of individual freedom*, like a woman's right to choose and marriage equality. Take another look at the Bill of Rights (the first ten amendments to the Constitution) and you will see it regards personal, individual freedoms *as against* a big government, not a statement of "Don't regulate giant corporations."

* * * * *

19

ALL "CONSERVATIVES" HATE AMERICA

Self-proclaimed "conservatives" (I dispute this use of the word to describe these people. They are, more accurately, big government Republicans) throw around words like "Marxism," "socialism," and "communism" without knowing what any of these words actually mean. For the record, communism means the people (the community, perhaps through government, but eventually government just melts away; at least, that is the *theory*) own "the means of production," which is a fascinating phrase. Socialism is a transitional phase on the road to communism. Communism ultimately describes being a classless and stateless society. *These* are the true meanings of these words. There are many books and other materials you can read to delve into this complex theoretical system created by Karl Marx, and later changed by others, but at least we now have a basic understanding of these words.

If you believe in the *private ownership* of "the means of production" (factories, businesses, and farms are excellent examples), then you are by definition *neither a communist nor a socialist*. They likewise use the word "capitalism" and imply or state that what we have *now*—a few gigantic corporations with global resources and impenetrable market domination—is actually "capitalism." The truth is, we are in the grips of crony, criminal, corporate plutocracy and oligarchy.

Upward social mobility (the heart of the American Dream) has slowed dramatically. "Capitalism" as a theory, though he didn't use the word, was outlined in and after 1776 by Scotsman Adam Smith in *The Wealth of Nations* (a very long and ponderous set of books, full of theory and pontification) and then added to and refined by others. It requires a lot of conditions to be met before a perfect competitive marketplace exists. Consumers must have full and complete information; there must be low barriers to enter the competitive marketplace; and a large group of relatively equally-sized competitors must be fighting for market share with a large number of buyers. *These* are the essential keys to such a market-based, capitalist economy. We do not have these absolutely essential predicates and thus we have a non-functional economy if you believe we are "capitalistic." Can you or I start an oil company to compete with Exxon/Mobil and BP? Can we start a competitor to VISA or MasterCard or create a chain to rival Wal-Mart?

What is laid before our eyes today is not "capitalism." It is a broken, warped and distorted version of capitalism like what we had in the late 1800s that was eventually broken up producing great results for America. We've had "antitrust laws" on the books since the 1890s because the excesses of "capitalism" became too much to bear—a massive concentration of disproportionate market power in the hands of far too few market participants.

When Republican President Teddy Roosevelt instigated "trust busting" in the first decade of the 1900s, he was hailed as a hero by the people and vilified by the monopolists. Convincing people that what we have now is *really* "capitalism" is another attempt to impose what Teddy Roosevelt and the people of his era knew was not capitalism. We are refighting the old war. The Kochs have taken us back in time. This is the current war on the economic front, and on the "social issues" front, the "conservatives" hate America too.

The sheep that support the Koch agenda are focused on social issues yet they do not understand the Constitution. True American values are diversity, acceptance, tolerance and freedom. The truth about self-declared "conservatives" is that they are arrogant, smug, ignorant and authoritarian. Not content with their First Amendment right to try to *persuade* people to live their private lives the way these "conservatives" want, they use a missionary zeal to grab onto their government as if it is their personal property—their toy, their play thing—to use as a hammer to bludgeon the rest of us into conforming to their compulsion of how life must be lived. Watching television and listening to radio indicates no shortage of religious programming. Driving around America shows no shortage of houses of worship. And yet, because the "conservatives" have not succeeded in compelling everyone to live as they demand, they are insisting that the government is their rightful possession, and we must all obey their dictates. Thus women's bodies are the property of others; marriage choice is at the discretion of the "conservatives"; what substances I incorporate into my body are not my choice; and when to end my life is some stranger's decision as well.

The Patriot Act is a fine example of how "small government" people love big government. Warrantless wiretapping; electronic snooping and eavesdropping; "national security letters" that have the effect of a subpoena but without any evidence of wrongdoing, any judicial involvement or anything else a government agent is curious to know about (like what library books you have checked out) are now legal in this authoritarian state, and the "conservatives" clamor for it to exist and persist. During the George W. Bush years, the federal government was caught tapping into the AT&T (and others) telephone and data streams without the knowledge or involvement of the court—no checks and balances, no oversight. They were wholesale spying on Americans in blatant violation of the Fourth Amendment to the Constitution. When lawsuits about this began to move forward, Congress retroactively immunized the government and the companies involved, and the lawsuits were dismissed.

When police plant GPS tracking units in the undercarriages of people's cars and track them for weeks without any court knowledge, approval or supervision; when government agents can break into a home without a warrant; when government spies can invade your privacy in a myriad of ways with no court knowledge or any evidence of wrongdoing, this is big government liberalism by the very definition of the "small government conservatives." The truth is, they love big government, when it comes to issues of authoritarianism and control of people's lives.

This group of characteristics (arrogance, smugness, ignorance and authoritarianism) is not only a dangerous combination, but a recipe for the end of America. Self-declared "conservatives" do not accept the essential, basic, most fundamental principle of America—freedom. They believe they have the God-granted power to decide public policy according to their religious and quasi-religious views. They believe they are the true and rightful inheritors of the American Revolution. They believe they have special rights to decide all issues for all of us and that government must use its power to compel all of us to obey their whims. They believe the rest of us have no role to play, that our only job is to pay taxes to pay for *their* play thing but that we do not have an *equal call on the protections of government or an equal call on the making of public policy.*

Perhaps even more fascinating is that these self-declared "conservatives" actually believe that they believe in "small government" while *simultaneously demanding very big government.* Using our examples from preceding paragraphs, whether it is two people in love deciding to marry; one person deciding in the privacy of home to smoke a joint; one person deciding to have an operation on her body; or one person deciding to exit this world just short of its otherwise inevitable conclusion to avoid horrendous pain, these self-declared "conservatives" *insist* that *they* get to make these decisions and *only they have the right to make these decisions.* Now *that* is smug and arrogant. Perhaps more fascinating still is that these self-declared "conservatives" do not think to analyze themselves. If they did, they would come to the realization they are demanding government intrude into places where government has no business being according to their own nostrums of "small government." Yet when it comes to economic regulation (where Article I, Section 8 of the Constitution says the government has every business being) they demand government has no role to play.

These self-declared "conservatives" proclaim loudly their love of the Constitution, but do not seem to understand the very document they adore, which has that hated word "regulate" in it. Nor do they understand the Supreme Court's decisions in interpreting the Constitution's "regulation of interstate commerce" cases. In short, these "conservatives" want government to *not* be involved in areas where government is explicitly *supposed* to be involved; and conversely, they want government deeply involved where it is expressly *not* supposed to be involved. This most crucial, basic contradiction is lost on them, and they get outraged and vomit up vileness when confronted with their hypocrisy.

While these self-declared "conservatives" have chanted the slogan "Obey the Constitution," they have far too little understanding of what the Constitution is *really* all about. The *Constitution is about government and only about government, primarily the federal government. Nowhere* does it proclaim America a capitalist country; nowhere does it say that a "free market system" is the economic system we will use. *It is simply not there.* Indeed, many of the original ten Constitutional amendments (called collectively "The Bill of Rights"), which passed in the time of the Constitution, made clear that people (not corporations but flesh-and-blood humans, called "natural persons" by the law) are free and are to be *left alone* to live their private lives as they see fit. People were to be free from unreasonable searches and seizures in the Fourth Amendment (and just what does *that* mean?) and were to be free of cruel and unusual punishment in the Eighth Amendment (have any idea what *that* means?). If "conservatives" hate government so much, yet simultaneously love the Founders and their Constitution so much, why did the Founders provide for *a government at all*, much less a government with significant power? The truth is, the Founders rebelled loudly against taxation without representation—once representation was provided, taxation was acceptable.

The "conservatives" have a fundamental misunderstanding of the Constitution. The Constitution is a guidebook of principles. The vast majority of the statements in the Constitution and its amendments are statements of principle. The Constitution is not a magical encyclopedia of specific factual answers to every specific factual question that can ever arise. If it were, the Constitution would be 20,000 pages or more. Besides, who can predict the future? Did George Washington, Thomas Jefferson and their generation envision cars, the Internet, telephones, satellites, television and radio, as well as all the other technological advances that occurred since their time like the cotton gin, telegraph and steam engine? Look at the Ninth Amendment: "The enumeration in the Constitution, of certain rights, shall not be construed to deny or disparage others retained by the people." What does *that* mean? Does it mean a woman has a right to control her own body; that people are free to smoke marijuana; that two people in love can marry? What does "Congress shall have the power to regulate commerce among the several states" mean? Does that mean a woman in California, growing marijuana in her backyard, carrying it into her living room and smoking it, is engaged in "interstate commerce"? Why do we even have courts if the Constitution automatically contains all the answers to every question that can ever arise? Incidentally, the Supreme Court ruled in *Raich v. Gonzalez* that the California woman growing her own reefer and keeping all the activity within a few hundred feet of her home was indeed engaged in interstate commerce and subject to Congressional regulation; this was dictated from 3,000 miles away in Washington, D.C.

The Constitution requires interpretation—*that* is why we have courts. The Founders did not know from telephones, airplanes, motor vehicles and the Internet. They did not then have a nation where crossing state lines was so easy or injecting matters into interstate commerce was done with a computer mouse click. The Supreme Court has, for almost 80 years now, interpreted the Constitution to give the federal government power to "regulate commerce among the several states" in such a way that a person growing marijuana in her own backyard and carrying it into her living room is "interstate commerce." Virtually anything is now "interstate commerce" and the *so-called conservatives on the Supreme Court have been leading that charge.* Self-declared "conservatives" do not know, or care to know, these things. Their utter lack of basic knowledge of either the Constitution or simple civics is breathtaking. Yet they scream loudly their opinions and demand, as bullies do, that they be obeyed. As seen through the eyes of the corporate special interests, these are suckers ripe for the fleecing, rubes just waiting to be manipulated.

What is at the heart of this matter is the brainwashing of these self-declared "conservatives" by the very powerful and monied interests represented by the Koch brothers (Charles and David) and people like Phillip Anschutz (a multi-billionaire real estate mogul) and Richard DeVos (the founder and king of the fortune created by Amway) as well as many other members of the "one percent club" who own and control vast amounts of wealth. These individuals, plus corporate interests like the oil industry, the banking industry, the pharmaceutical industry and the insurance industry have a *very real* economic stake in hobbling government, and in disabling government from acting as a counterbalance, a countervailing force, to provide reasonable regulation and stop predatory business practices that harm consumers and destroy the economy.

The monied interests have done a masterful job of brainwashing these self-declared "conservatives" into believing that "small government" means *economic anarchy and no government regulation of big business,* and yet *"small government" means massive government regulation of peoples' private lives.* The monied interests have done this by merging concepts like "freedom and liberty" with "government is the problem" and manipulate the words "small business" when they mean "big business" and mix in vague but "good" sounding words like "job creators" and "job crushing government regulation." By manipulating words to evoke images stored in our DNA (images of antipathy towards government and individual entrepreneurs going forth to build empires from nothing) and carefully, masterfully directing these self-declared "conservatives" to think *superficially*, and simply confuse "regulation of commerce among the several states" (Article I, Section 8 of the Constitution) with "job crushing regulation," the monied interests have converted millions of poor and working class people to their very hostile cause.

The pharmaceutical industry wants to get drugs to market and charge whopping prices for them. They also want *government* to pay for them (through Medicare and Medicaid) and health insurance companies to pay for them at top dollar. These same drug companies want to get drugs to market so they can make fabulous profits but without having to take responsibility for drugs that kill or injure people. They also want to hide test results that show their drugs are dangerous. Only a properly working Food and Drug Administration (government) can stand in their way. The banks want to charge 30% interest on credit cards and car dealers want to charge 30% on auto loans. Payday loan companies want to charge 400% interest to trap poor people into a cycle of debt and fees that create wealth for payday lenders. These special interests do not want anyone telling them they cannot rip off their victims. Only a properly working government agency can stop these practices. Oil companies want to "Drill, baby, drill" yet do not want anyone telling them they cannot destroy the Gulf of Mexico with deepwater oil-drilling blowouts. Oil companies do not want to pay for damages when the Exxon Valdez runs aground; Chevron does not want to pay when it ruins the rain forest in the Amazon. Only properly working government agencies are strong enough (potentially) and comprehensive enough to stand in the way of private special interests harming the environment, people's health and the public interest.

Private interests care about private interests. This simple statement should not be shocking. Government's role is to look at the broader, public interest. It may be a wonderful thing for BP's bank accounts to "Drill, baby, drill" in the Gulf of Mexico and extract vast fortunes from it. But it is not in the public interest to have unsafe drilling methods used that cause massive blowouts and oil spills. It is in the public interest to *not destroy* the Gulf of Mexico. It certainly is good for the finances of Bank of America, Citigroup and other large banks to sell mortgages to people who have no way to pay for them, who are not qualified for them and will default on them, and then lie to investors about the nature of the bonds that have these mortgages mixed together in them. It is also good for these banks to have "bond rating agencies" in their pockets to tell investors these toxic bonds are top notch material. It is not good for the public interest to have massive amounts of defaults and foreclosures, and a collapsed housing market. It is very good for AIG's owners to make vast fortunes selling insurance to other gigantic corporations to insure their business gambles. It is not good for the public interest to have AIG be so big and so entangled in everything so that when it collapses, the entire economy is brought crashing down.

These simple examples of a proper government role in fulfilling the Article I, Section 8 Constitutional duty to "regulate commerce among the several states" make big business *very* unhappy. They want to do *whatever* it is they want, and with no government "interference." So they have hired image makers, wordsmiths and symbol manipulators to transform *their* corporate hopes and dreams into the political goals of their *victims*. By merging simplistic slogans with powerful images akin to "mom and apple pie," these skilled charlatans have brainwashed people into *wanting* drugs that will kill them; banks that will *fleece* them; oil companies that will *steal* from them *and* destroy the world of their descendants. By skillfully manipulating unsophisticated people, the monied interests have made *government* the enemy and *big business* the good guy. The truth is the reverse.

The truth is that "government" is supposed to be "small" when it comes to invading people's homes and life choices. "Government" is supposed to be "small" when it comes to using religion to establish public policy. Take a look at the very first words of the First Amendment: "Congress shall make no law respecting an establishment of religion." Did the Founders make these the *first words* of the *First* Amendment by random accident, or were these words *really* important? Did the Founders intend for government to stay out of religion so that religion would not be jammed down the throats of the American people? Isn't what these self-declared "conservatives" want *precisely* what the first words of the First Amendment condemn? When these self-declared "conservatives" declare that "America is a Christian country" (which they do often) and try to impose their own version of religion on the rest of us through public laws, is this not making law "respecting an establishment of religion"? When these self-declared "conservatives" deny the very words of Article I, Section 8 of the Constitution, giving Congress the power to *regulate* interstate commerce, who is it that hates America? Who is it that does the opposite of what the Constitution states? Who wants "small government" to be "big government" when it comes to the areas where "small government" is the Constitutional requirement; and who wants "small government" when "big government" is *explicitly* allowed in the very Constitution these self-declared "conservatives" declare they love so much? Who does not know up from down? Who has been so brainwashed that their professed love of America has become hate for America by hating what the Constitution declares we should love, and loving what the Constitution declares is a fundamental proper role of government?

* * * * *

I AM A BETTER
"CONSERVATIVE" THAN
MOST "CONSERVATIVES"

As I have said, "conservatives" hate America. Indeed, they are not "conservatives." They are America-hating radicals. How do we *know* they are America-hating radicals? They have taken the Constitution, turned it upside down, defined it as the opposite of what it is, and tried to implement a vision that is expressly rejected by the Constitution, all the while claiming to act *in the name of* the Constitution. *That* is hating America. *That* is hating the Constitution. *That* is a brainwashing by the monied interests who want people to believe the Constitution is everything it is not.

I am the real conservative, so is the American Civil Liberties Union. I, and my allegedly "progressive" or "liberal" friends, understand the Constitution (we have actually studied it— what a concept!) and adhere to its "original intent" far more closely than these self-declared "conservatives." It is part of the brainwashing of the "conservatives" by the monied interests to label the ACLU as "radical" and "subversive" and "un-American." A key part of the brainwashing is to convince people that *they* are the true inheritors of the Constitution; that *they* are the real definers of what the Constitution means. The fact that their definitions and ideas are directly contradicted by the Constitution simply means the monied interests had their work cut out for them. And give them credit—they and their puppets have done a masterful job tricking millions of people into not only embracing the opposite of the Constitution, but then fighting for the destruction of their own economic interests in favor of their masters. A key part of the manipulation is through the use of religion.

Religion is a very personal matter. The First Amendment to the Constitution reads, in full: "Congress shall make no law respecting an establishment of religion, or prohibiting the free exercise thereof; or abridging the freedom of speech, or of the press; or the right of the people peaceably to assemble, and to petition the Government for a redress of grievances." Lots of good stuff in there, no? Look at all the different rights in there, separated by commas. Let's focus on the Congressional prohibition and free exercise parts for now. By the way, each of these phrases, inside each of the commas, is called a "clause" in court and lawyer-speak. When you hear lawyers and judges talking about "clauses" in the Constitution or Amendments, this is what they mean—the distinct pieces, the separate concepts stated in a place with other concepts but separated by commas from the *other* distinct conceptual phrases surrounding it. Thus, the "due process clause" of the Fourteenth Amendment or the "equal protection clause" of the Fourteenth Amendment are parts of the overall (and longer) Fourteenth Amendment, but are distinct pieces which the courts pluck out, examine and apply individually. The First Amendment has the "free exercise clause," the "establishment clause" and so on.

In the First Amendment, the first two clauses do two very big things: The first clause prohibits Congress from making any law "respecting an establishment of religion" and the second clause prevents Congress from "prohibiting the free exercise" of religion. Taken together, the message is unmistakable: Congress (meaning the federal government, since Congress is the lawmaking body of the federal government) must stay out of religion and let the people do what they want with religion. Religion is a very personal matter. The Colonists did not like the King of England having an official state religion— the Anglican Church—and thus the First Amendment has an historical backdrop. Today and throughout American history, religionists have attempted to use their religion to make laws and create (and enforce) public policy. "The Women's Christian Temperance Movement" should tell you all you need to know about some of the founders of the movement created to make liquor illegal in the United States; a movement, incidentally, that resulted in the Eighteenth Amendment, itself repealed by the Twenty-First Amendment.

Attempts to take one or another's religious views and impose them on the rest of America is an old habit for us. That these attempts are also un-Constitutional (literally) should also be apparent. It is not the place of the *government* to make laws respecting an establishment of religion. It is up to each person to run his or her own life based upon his or her own religious views, or not. That is the First Amendment "free exercise" clause. So I ask you: Who is the true "conservative"? Is it me, or someone attempting to import their religious views into the law, and then use the hammer of "big government" to compel us *all* to live by *their* religious views?

This is one reason why I say, "I am a better conservative than most conservatives." *They* seem to mean "old time local community values" when *they* say "conservative." They want those *perceived* "old time local community values" to be locked forever into law and made the public policy of the land to be enforced by a big government hand. The fact that Thomas Jefferson cheated on his wife and had children with slaves, i.e., Sally Hemmings, (as is true of many of the Founders who owned slaves) does not seem to factor into the "old time local community values" of these self-proclaimed "conservatives." Maybe in keeping with the tradition, so many of these "old time values" types also frequent prostitutes, are gay or cheat on their spouses.

These self-proclaimed "conservatives" with their religious zealotry have every right to preach their religious zealotry, which is why we have the "free speech clause" of the First Amendment. When I drive around America, I see no shortage of houses of worship. When I turn on the television or tune around the radio dial, I see and hear no shortage of religious broadcasters attempting to persuade me of the righteousness of their cause. And this is all to the good. The point of the First Amendment's free speech clause ("Congress shall make no law…abridging the freedom of speech") is to protect the right to speak. That should be obvious. The way our system was set up was to provide a very wide, very robust space, lots of elbow room, for free speech to reign. The courts have called it "the marketplace of ideas" and have jealously guarded it (and properly so, in my humble opinion) as was intended by the Founders. If someone can *persuade* someone else to run his or her life by this or that set of religious principles, so be it. That is up to the marketplace of ideas, the free speech of people and the individual freedom and liberty to make up one's own mind. Government has no role to play there, and that is the way the Founders intended it. So when I adhere to the original intent of the Constitution and the self-proclaimed "conservatives" do not, I ask again: Who is the real "conservative"?

"Government" is a legitimate force. The Founders created a government to set public policy. Government is here to lead and to regulate for the public interest. Government is here for all the people; it is not the property of a few. Government is here to look out for the general, broad interest, not the narrow views of greed heads and religious charlatans. To get rid of government is to invite chaos.

* * * * *

21

THEIR DIABOLICAL PLAN
TO DESTROY AMERICA

Give the extremist radical corporatists their due: They are a finely-honed, military-style machine. They want economic anarchy and they are getting it. They are top-down and they whip their troops into shape with mind-control manipulation, but their dupes like it that way. Playing off of "manly" images of self-reliance, "go-it-alone" toughness and base, nativist babble, the corporatists have the formula for manipulating their suckers. To reinforce the message daily and keep their troops marching, look at their interconnected parts: a 24 hour, 7 day a week cable television propaganda machine; a network of powerful talk radio stations; a thick grove of well-funded think tanks that churn out people and positions to advance their ideology; and a ruthlessly enforced orthodoxy that accepts no dissent. When Newt Gingrich attacked Rep. Paul Ryan's plan to privatize and destroy Medicare, the entire machine jumped on Gingrich and pummeled him back into the fold within a very short time. Indeed, Gingrich was forced onto his knees to seek forgiveness, as a supplicant. *This* is a powerful machine.

When we step back and look at the sheer size and scope of the machine, it is breathtaking: Big money boys and owners of media communication conglomerates, all linked together by sheer greed and the ideology to feed greed, each play their part in saturating America with their ideology. And the idea is to trick millions of people into adopting a global corporate agenda (mixed with heaping doses of misstated religion as justification) that intends the end of America as we know it.

In 2011, when state after state adopted nearly identical union-busting tactics and laws, that was no accident. Indiana, Michigan, Ohio, Wisconsin, New Jersey and elsewhere were all being programmed by the people described above and all fed through another of their front groups: ALEC. ALEC (the American Legislative Exchange Council) is an organization funded by gigantic corporations like State Farm, Coors (you like beer?), Chevron, the former Phillip Morris tobacco company (now re-named Altria Group, I think to sound like "altruism") and the ubiquitous Koch brothers to create model legislation which gets introduced in the states and rammed through to enact a corporatist agenda. ALEC is not new—it was founded four decades ago and plays a key role in the machine that we are dissecting here.

ALEC, Fox Boobs, the radio airwaves saturation are all part of the playbook envisioned long ago and patiently put in place by the various constituent members of the group that now dominates America. It is a natural alliance: Wall Street wants no regulation; the Koch brothers want no regulation (their companies and industry are among the top emitters of air pollution—why would they want government regulation and environmental protection?); all of them (broadcast companies and all) want to pay no taxes, and they all know that the only force large enough, powerful enough and with the staying power of an institution (it doesn't die) is *government*. Government, like Exxon, is an artificial thing. It lives long after the people who inhabit it at any given time are dead. Government (especially the *federal government*) has tremendous resources fed by hundreds of billions in tax revenue, and can act as a counterbalance to the predations of the corporatists. With federal courts, federal prosecutors and a huge workforce, the federal government is the natural predator of Wall Street, the Koch brothers and the broadcasters since it can jail them, take away their licenses to broadcast, and impose rules on them—rules they do not like. As nature has balance, for a long time, business had balance. Government regulated business and kept it in check. That balanced relationship ended in 1981 with the election of Ronald Reagan ("government is the problem") and has become more unbalanced ever since.

Is it any wonder *hatred* of the *federal government* is the number one thing being promoted by the Republicon Party? This is how they get economic anarchy: emasculate the federal government's ability to stand in their way. Ginned up by the Michele Bachmanns, the Ronald Reagans, and the entirety of Republicon Party orthodoxy, the famous quote from Grover Norquist says it all: "I don't want to abolish government. I simply want to reduce it to the size where I can drag it into the bathroom and drown it in the bathtub." Their goal, through their puppet spokespeople on television, radio and in politics (let's not forget John Boehner, Mitch McConnell and the rest, all beating the same "hate the federal government" drum), is to kill the only natural predator that can keep their population in check, like animals in nature keep each other from overrunning the environment.

All of this did not happen overnight. It took decades of careful planning and a few strokes of luck—the Koch brothers did not invent Rupert Murdoch, he came along on his own but was meshed into the big plan—to make this all happen. And they have natural advantages: continuing streams of vast amounts of money from big business and a shared ideology of no taxes on the rich and no regulation of big business, that is, themselves. They want economic anarchy.

The simplicity of their plan is genius. They don't care, or have to care, about abortion, prayer in the public schools or other "social issues" like marriage equality and gun control. They can play to these issues and get the "base" to evaluate politics and politicians from an *entirely different scale of analysis*, i.e. the social issues matter and the economic issues do not. What you and I under appreciate is that, while we focus on the money, the power, and control mechanisms that I have described, the other side's "base" uses a *whole different scorecard—they* care about where politicians stand on social issues. *Their measuring stick is entirely different*. It's like playing one game but each side has totally different rules. That is why Sarah Palin, Michele Bachmann, Rick Santorum and the other purveyors of Christian hate resonate so well with the "vote values" people. Their base is not interested in the money and regulation of power, they accept as gospel (literally) that whatever companies are here now *are* the "free market," and "freedom and liberty" means leave business alone. They never stop to think that "big government" can mean anything *other than* "interference with business" while you and I know that interference with our personal lives is precisely the kind of "big government" the Constitution and Bill of Rights was designed to control and keep "small." It simply does not matter to them that big business is so dominant—*that is outside their field of vision*. They are evaluating the world from an entirely different perspective, a perspective that is religion-based and fear-driven. Focusing on "the war on terror" and "Muslim extremism" while also seeking out the "pro-life" candidates and those who will "protect marriage" and keep "government from taking your gun away," these people actually elevate to *top importance* people who will exult "American Exceptionalism" and "We're Number 1."

The Koch brothers, Rupert Murdoch and their ilk know all of this and play it all like a master violinist. How we can reach these people is a topic many of us have puzzled over for a long time. In my humble opinion, we have not reached a proper answer. The best answer I can come up with is to out organize them, out work them, out hustle them and remember that there are more of us than there are of them. The challenge for us is to find our people, organize them and keep them motivated. That is not nearly as easy as it sounds, especially when the Democratic Party is busy chasing after the same monied interests that fund the Republicons.

* * * * *

22
IS IT THE END OF
THE BEGINNING OR
THE BEGINNING OF THE END?

Their goals have reached fruition, but not completely. There are still taxes on the rich and regulations on big business. Not enough taxation or regulation to work for most Americans, but from the Koch perspective, too much. It took time and a step-by-step advance for the Kochs and their ilk to get here. What seemed unimaginable once is now accepted and standard practice. Ronald Reagan, considered extreme in 1980, is now far too moderate for the current crop of 'Cons. Reagan raised taxes; made deals with Democrats to shore up Social Security; made government bigger; and "cut and ran" from Lebanon when an interventionist, militaristic foreign policy met with 241 deaths of Marines at a bombed barracks.

I was nine years-old in 1968 when Ronald Reagan ran for president. He was a joke. I did not know who he was. I had never seen a Ronald Reagan movie, didn't even know what a "B" movie was, but I was aware enough to know he was beyond the fringe of acceptable politics in 1968. Twelve years later, he was President of the United States. Do you honestly think that happened by accident or evolution? Or was it the relentless work of a committed, focused and monied group that set out with a plan to accomplish a goal?

From Reagan of the 1980s with his message of "Government isn't the solution to our problems, government *is* the problem" to Mitch McConnell and the Tea Party crazies of today, we can trace a direct line. Reagan spoke out against taxes; today's Republicons have converted "no new taxes" into a *theology*, such that even removing tax deductions for corporate jets and yachts is considered (by them) a "tax increase" and thus unacceptable. Reagan *could have* tried that message in the 1980s, but he would have been going too far too fast for America. The natural end result—the furthest conclusion of this ideology, this theology ,taking his arguments to their logical and extreme end—is where we are today, but it took *conditioning* of the American mind to get a big chunk of the populace there today. That conditioning has now occurred and millions of people now accept as an article of faith that "Government is bad" and "Business is good" and that "Freedom and liberty = no regulation of business." So the question for you and me is: Will this relentless march to Koch-ism persist, or will the Occupy Wall Street movement and a Great Awakening right the ship and restore sanity to America? The answer is up to us and nothing is inevitable.

* * * * *

23

THE CHICKENS HAVE COME HOME TO ROOST, OCCUPY WALL STREET

The Bush torture memos and the lies that got us into Iraq are but two things that finally helped discredit the illegal Bush regime, as well as the "greed is good" mentality of Ronald Reagan and the years afterward (as exemplified by the movie *Inside Job*). Corporate trial lawyers cheating and lying, helped by a blatantly political Supreme Court majority, has woken people up to the need to rein in the politicized Supreme Court. The inequality and growing income disparity in America where 400 people own more than the bottom half of the population (150 *million* people *combined*) has galvanized regular Americans to see that politics is crucial and, indeed, politics is everything.

I believe people have largely figured much of this out for themselves. They may not be able to articulate it, and they may not have a lot of the facts and details in mind but viscerally, they sense what I am saying here is true. Indeed, the original Tea Party was based upon hatred of the bailouts. America was almost unanimous in despising those bailouts and despising the corporate titans who stole the economy and caused the Crash of 2008. What occurred next was disgusting, and fascinating. The Tea Partiers were almost immediately turned from hatred of the bailouts to *love for those who got the bailouts*; turned by having their attention turned to *hating the government that did the bailing out, instead of the banks that got bailed out.*

While writing this book, Occupy Wall Street happened. What I described above has now translated into a mass movement. Yet in contrast to our scattered and haphazard messaging (and the nascent Occupy Wall Street movement), for the Koch brothers and their ilk, they knew that inculcating their propaganda would take relentless focus and relentless repetition across multiple platforms—television, newspapers, radio, the Internet and the water cooler—from multiple mouths over an extended period of time. So they seeded magazines, newspapers and all other means of communication with their talking points, their talking heads and their messaging. They did not give up out of frustration or impatience; they merely kept feeding the machine and growing the machine, advancing their march step-by-step, over many years. Look at their advance over a sweep of time: In the late 1960s and into the 1970s, they played the culture wars to convert the South; they cozied up to the Moral Majority and the religious zealots; they looked for and nurtured candidates (Ronald Reagan, anyone?) who would advance their business agenda. But when Republicans like Bob Dole, Howard Baker, Bob Michel (who for years was the Republican *minority* leader of the House of Representatives) and other moderates did not advance the Koch agenda, the Kochs did not quit in frustration, they waited out the aging older moderates and created the new crop of crazies who would eventually take their place. Thus, Newt Gingrich, Tom DeLay, Jim DeMint, Tom Coburn; James ("Global warming is a hoax") Inhofe, Michele ("Global warming is a hoax") Bachmann and the rest of the numerous lunatic fringe eventually displaced the more moderate, more accommodating Republicans. This is what can happen if you give yourself the luxury of time, billions of dollars and work assiduously to advance your goals with a long-time horizon.

* * * *

24
WHERE ARE THE DEMOCRATS WHILE ALL THIS IS HAPPENING?

The Democratic Party must take a large share of the blame for our current conditions. Constantly retreating in the face of the focused, relentless bullying of the Republicon Party, the Koch brothers, their money, their friends' money, and their propaganda machine has helped legitimize their pushing strategy and their talking points, framing the debate to their liking. We did not challenge their "pro life" claim, neither challenging them to be "anti-war" nor pacifist (thus not "pro life") and not against the death penalty. We simply adopted their language instead of calling them "anti-women" or "anti-freedom" or "anti-choice" or "anti-abortion." On this point, incidentally, I have another example of us attacking each other over everything. When I call the 'Cons "anti-abortion," I get *our own language police* on me telling me, "We're all anti-abortion"! Can we remember for a moment who the enemy is here? Must the purity extend so deep on our side?

The Democratic Party should be winning every election, both nationally and in every state. The Democratic Party, standing for simple, basic, American principles and values, should present itself as a stark contrast to Republicons, and aggressively challenge the 'Cons to expose them for the frauds they are.

To do this, for us to win again, we need a strategy. We start with a simple question: *What do we stand for?* It's a profound and important question: *What are our defining, core principles?* We should agree on a short list of *really* important things on which we all can agree. We must then submerge all our other differences and disagreements in order to stay relentlessly focused on the big ticket items. This presents a problem, as our list is long. Social issues are important—gay rights, marriage equality, a woman's privacy—these are wedge issues that play into the hands of the other side by ginning up their base. Yet we cannot ignore them as we have to protect and further the freedoms and rights of all people. But what we *can* do is *emphasize.* By emphasizing economic issues, we can focus on issues that transcend current party politics and reach a broad spectrum of Americans. We can do what Bill Clinton did on abortion, "It should be safe, legal and rare," and move along.

I suggest *an economic populist agenda,* delivered with memorable sound bite phrases and relentless messaging. Thus "tax fairness" and "corporate welfare" should be injected into the lexicon at *every opportunity.* "Tax cheating billionaires," "coddling corporate criminals" and "Wall Street greed" get *everyone* riled up. "No more bailouts" will win near universal acclaim. "Outsourcing American jobs" is something most Americans hate. *Relentless use of these exact words across every platform, every day, is crucial to re-position and re-brand our party for what we represent.*

We should stick to a few simple, broadly agreed upon themes:

1. Tax fairness
2. End corporate welfare

3. Punish outsourcing of jobs
4. Scale back the global empire we have built
5. Punish waste fraud and abuse of tax dollars
6. Punish corporate criminality

There is our agenda. It will get far more than 50% of the people voting for it every time. If we add more items, we get more divided. We should minimize or downplay the other issues—emphasize that our nation's *very survival hinges on doing these few big things.*

Branding the Democratic Party (in much the same way "Scotch tape" and "Xerox this document" mean "Put adhesive tape on" and "Make a photocopy of this paper") as synonymous with these seven things—a short list of instantly popular, readily repeatable and easily memorized points—is a big start. *We have let the other side brand us.* The Democratic Party has become the party of gelatin desserts—weak, spineless and jiggly. It has allowed the Republicons to brand Democrats as "Jell-O." They have associated us with "socialism," "tax and spend," "big, bloated government," "wasting taxpayers' money," "coddling welfare queens," "supporting fringe weirdos like 'the gays'," and associating us with "un-American and anti-American views." They have laid claim to patriotism and symbols like the flag and the Bible for themselves exclusively. They have relentlessly associated themselves with religion and patriotic symbols like the military. They have arrogantly proclaimed that they, and only they, are the *true inheritors of the American Revolution.* They have arrogantly proclaimed that they, and only they, are the *true definers of what the Bible teaches.* They have arrogantly proclaimed that they, and only they, are the *true inheritors and defenders of the Constitution.*

It is no coincidence that President Obama has been relentlessly attacked as born elsewhere, foreign, and "not one of us." The same can be said of their attacks on the Democratic Party. We are accused of wanting "European-style socialism" and holding "un-American" views. These attacks are not random or by accident. It is the defining of *them* as "American" and us as "not American" that is then complemented by the symbols of God and country to make a complete picture that gets beaten into the brains of Americans. Recall my conversation with New Mexico Governor Bill Richardson at the Democratic National Convention in 2004. He awkwardly proved how inept the Democrats are at simply defining their core value and message.

I suggest an additional strategy, which we can run simultaneously with the re-branding/re-positioning strategy for the Democratic Party. That is, to *push* (I use that word intentionally) the Republicons into ever more extreme positions and *highlight* their ever more extreme positions. Here are issues with which to "push" them:

1. An aggressive push to bring jobs back to America by not using the tax code to subsidize outsourcing jobs, and actively punish outsourcers with extra taxes
2. An aggressive push for a balanced budget by ending corporate welfare
3. An aggressive push for taxing the rich—tax fairness
4. An aggressive push for punishing corporate criminals
5. An aggressive push for funding public education
6. An aggressive push for clean energy

This will divide them. It will force them to defend corporate greed, environmental destruction and tax unfairness. If we use personal stories of rampant cancer tied to pollution, we can bring the message home: "We need to stop living in a toxic stew of chemicals and pollution." It will get them squabbling just as they use flag-burning, gun control, and abortion and gay rights to get us squabbling. We can use "hot button" issues that get the Tea Party riled up to split their side—push them into fratricide. They do it to us constantly; turnabout is fair play!

Then we must not be afraid when they get what looks like a lot of adherents to their ever more extreme views. It is crucial to remember that America has over 300 million people in it. Even excluding people under 18, according to the Census, it's still 225 million adults. So when Fox Boobs, which tops out at 3 million viewers, is getting roughly one and a half percent of America watching, these are *not* big numbers. Roughly 70 million people voted for President Obama, and roughly 60 million voted for Senator John McCain. The gap of votes between them alone was more than three times the entire highest watched Fox Boobs program!

We need to remember that, in such a large country with such a large population, the *visibility* of a small group of kooks and freaks does *not* a majority make! As we *push* the other side into ever more extreme positions—highlighting their "support-the-corporations-at-all-costs" philosophy, their "support-outsourcing-American-jobs," and "coddle-corporate-criminals" attitude—they will *continue* to have adherents. We *cannot* let that scare us. We need to focus on issues that the *broad millions of people agree on* like tax fairness, ending corporate welfare, downsizing the empire, stopping the outsourcing of American jobs, balancing the budget intelligently, prosecuting waste, fraud and abuse of both tax dollars and by Wall Street, and not coddling corporate criminals by sucking up to Wall Street. In this age of instant everything, where we all have acquired attention deficit disorder (AADD), where we all need to be "bottom lined" in 20 seconds or we tune out, it is crucial to communicate as the other side does, with quick, memorable sound bites that *evoke and trigger an entire set of thoughts, beliefs and values in two seconds.* That is the new, modern game of political communication and we had better master it fast. They sure have, and look at the results. In short: Stay broad, stay popular and stay populist!

※ ※ ※ ※ ※

THE DEMOCRATIC PARTY "LEADERSHIP" IS WEAK AND CORRUPT

The rank-and-file of the Democratic Party is a good, solid base of middle class people who understand the balance that is needed to have a strong, stable society. A proper government, as envisioned by the Founders, keeps an eye on, and a hand against, the excesses of people, including people *within* government. A proper government is also one that is small when intruding on people's individual life choices—their freedom and liberty. A proper government, as set out by the Founders, is one where no one needs to worry about their phone being tapped, their computer bugged or their library books monitored, at least without the checks and balances of a judge holding the government to its evidentiary standard stated in the Fourth Amendment to the Constitution.

Women control their own bodies, two people in love can marry, Bill Maher can smoke all the reefer he wants (whether for medicinal reasons, recreational reasons or no reason at all) and people can control when and how they exit this world. Speaking up for clear, concise principles—like proper regulation of interstate commerce and a fair tax code—is what the Democratic Party *should* be doing. However, this current version of the Democratic Party is spineless and hobbled by being beholden to many of the same corporate interests that control the Republicon Party.

Since the 1970s, the Democratic Party has not figured out what it stands *for* and what it stands *against*. This confusion is seen by its support of "free trade" deals that no Democratic Party should be supporting—it outsources our jobs. It is seen when Democrats agree to the Bush tax cuts; when adopting the language of "uncertainty" as in "assuring the marketplace that there will not be uncertainty"; and when agreeing with the fundamental concept of the 'Cons that *the job of government is to serve the interests of business, especially big business.* The job of government is to serve the interests of *the American people*, not business interests. There is *nothing* in the Constitution consecrating a capitalist or corporatist system as our economic system. To the contrary, Congress is given the explicit power to *regulate* interstate commerce. The Democratic Party caves in when faced with fierce aggression by the 'Cons on social issues—Democrats have to mimic the "tough on crime" line of the 'Cons. Democrats have to go along with the Hyde Amendment banning all federal funds for abortion. Democrats must acquiesce to the global war empire lest they be "soft" on (take your pick) communism, terrorism, or any other "ism" the 'Cons concoct as the flavor-of-the-month. Democrats have abandoned the effort to regulate firearms, thus allowing massive carnage in our streets. Even simple, sensible gun regulation is a forbidden topic for Democrats. They have been cowed.

Being "Republicon-lite" (half the fat cat of our regular Republicon) is *not* a winning formula. As Harry Truman said, "Given the choice between a Republican and someone who acts like a Republican, people will vote for the real Republican all the time." Yet Bill Clinton and his Democratic Leadership Council (DLC) consciously turned the Democratic Party into precisely this 'Con-lite version. Bob Dole, running against Clinton in the 1996 presidential race, could not gain traction because Clinton had moved so close to the Republican Party that Dole was running against a different version of himself. This trend has continued.

The Democratic Party has become so broad that it *cannot* stand for much of anything. From "Blue Dogs" like Ben Nelson in the Senate and Heath Shuler in the House to formerly traditional Democrats like Russ Feingold and Barbara Boxer, the Democratic Party is so rife with internal dissent and so compromised by the drive for campaign cash (from the same corporate interests as the 'Cons) that the Democrats are incapable of governing responsibly. That is to say, the leadership is incapable of governing. They are afraid of attacks by the 'Cons; afraid of offending the monied corporate interests; and assembled from so many different groups (i.e., gays, blacks, unions) that it cannot manage its own coalition. Add to this the need to attract independents who have sworn off both parties (yet are actually simply ping-ponging between the parties), and the Democratic Party is frozen into inaction.

Further proof is how the Democratic Party has treated (or rather, mistreated) unions. In truth, the Democratic Party *should* be called "The Labor Party" as it is in many other countries. Claiming to represent the interests of working people, the Democratic Party fails miserably. While singing sweet songs into their ears, the Democratic Party, once in power, does very little for the unions. Feeding off their money and their volunteers, the Democratic Party rides to victory, then makes deals that actively hurt the very unions they just rode to get into office. The unions, for their part, have viewed the Democrats as less awful than the "scary Republicons." The Democratic Party has played this up, using the boogeyman of the 'Cons to scare money and support from the unions. "Look at those awful Republicans," the Democrats say, "They really hate you and will destroy you." "It's either us or destruction," say the Democrats to the unions, and the unions have bought it for decades. The death-of-a-thousand-cuts now being inflicted on the unions is the natural result of a Democratic Party too weak to actually stand up for the unions, which form its natural base.

Look at the assault on public employee unions launched by the Republicons in the states recently. Where has the Democratic Party been? Invisible is where—no actual nor even *verbal* public support. The Democrats cannot even muster the strength to argue, "Did the unions cause the Crash of 2008? Did the unions steal all the money? Did the unions sell fraudulent sub-prime mortgages to people and then package them up and sell them with lies causing a huge fraudulent bubble that burst and melted us all down?" The Democratic Party leadership cannot even do *that*. It is sad to conclude that the current "leadership" of the institution that is the Democratic Party is pathetic. This doesn't mean we have to give up on the institution that is the Democratic Party, but we need to reclaim it and dispense with the current crop of lousy "leaders." The Democratic Party has been around since the 1820s, and has had many changes in philosophy and policy during that time. I don't recommend abandoning the Democratic Party because the current people who head it are not worthy of their posts; however, the question of how to re-take the Democratic Party is addressed in the next chapter.

The weakness of the current Democratic Party has led the unions to begin (finally) to re-think their unwavering support—and not a moment too soon. Howard Schaitberger, President of the International Association of Firefighters, has been the leader in publicly challenging the Democratic Party to do their jobs, and he should be joined by others.

Large numbers of people are turned off by the tweedle-dee, tweedle-dum style of politics we have now—two corporatist political parties that (especially on economic issues) serve the same set of masters; support the same corrupt tax code; support the same corrupt economic policies that send jobs overseas; and feed a global war empire that kills our citizens and gobbles up monstrous amounts of our national treasure. What is needed is a *new politics*—a politics devoid of labels— that focus on issues with a collection of issue statements and beliefs that are clear, concise and strongly implemented.

❀ ❀ ❀ ❀ ❀

26
A NEW POLITICS WITH
A NEW ENERGY

We need a fresh way of doing politics in America. The stale old politics has suppressed voter turnout and bred widespread cynicism. Especially in a democracy, widening the distance between the people and the government is fatal to stability and acceptance of rule. We need a new mix of issues that displaces the old strictures. We need clear, simple principles as well as clear, straightforward policy positions that focus on problems and solutions not labels triggered by one or a few words, which evoke different (false) images and mislead people. We need to renew our common set of *values* and define what they are. We need to articulate and fight for principles that resonate with people, like giving and getting a hand up, not a hand out; being honest; supporting hard work; respecting others; having a sense of fairness; having a sense of proportion. These are traits that apply universally. They can, and should, apply to our political system. It will lend genuineness to our new politics. There is also nothing wrong with having a belief in science *and* religion; a sense of wonder about life and this world; using your brain, and being able to look at yourself as others see you. These are all skills that make our lives better and make us better people, citizens, neighbors, co-workers, friends and spouses. We need to explain and understand these things as key to a pluralistic society, as American values. What is important is communicating to people more than just simple, meaningless slogans. We need to truly *connect* with people on a more fundamental, visceral level. People are sensing a breakdown in society and they need this anxiety addressed as part of a larger dialogue about policy solutions. For those who only want policy solutions, we need to have our talking points down—the statements of policy that communicate (quickly and clearly) where we stand, and in a substantive, not misleading or treacherous, way.

* * * * *

27
PERSONAL RESPONSIBILITY
AND ETHICS

The Republicons have done a fine job of turning the phrase "personal responsibility" into a guided missile, a weapon used to devastate their perceived enemies. They demand we "blame ourselves" for our failings, while giving a pass to all manner of corporate criminality. If it is wrong to lie to a spouse about an affair, it is wrong to lie to the public about spending money on a "global war on terror" when that "global war on terror" is actually a money laundering, corporate welfare scam. Cheating is cheating and not something to aspire to, or to teach others to do. It is unacceptable to blame victims of fraud and criminality for their plight when they have been cheated, and reward the cheaters while *simultaneously* claiming to speak with moral authority, given by God, no less. When I practiced law, I saw all manner of dishonesty—blatant lying, hiding evidence, setting up ambushes based on falsified evidence. I saw very little accountability, and I see this every day in the broader areas of life outside the court room—the business world, politics, interpersonal relations. I hate to sound like a crotchety old man or a church lady (thank *you,*

Dana Carvey) but I see a major lack of basic human decency and it concerns me greatly. I am not alone. There is a deep-seated yearning in America for a return to basic principles of rectitude and honesty. Sadly, we often exempt ourselves from these requirements while demanding them from everyone else, and we get angry when others violate these rules. Just so long as it is everyone *else* practicing these, we give *ourselves* a pass. Don't get me wrong, I have my failings and I have done people wrong along the way. I am my harshest critic and remind myself of my failings constantly. It is a hard way to live, but that's how I live. I whip myself for past mistakes and berate myself to make myself better. I have tried mightily to learn from my mistakes, the mistakes of others, and to be better in the future. No one achieves perfection, but we all should try to strive for it. We all need to hold ourselves accountable and not give ourselves a free pass from the rules of basic decency and honesty simply because we are us, and it is all right for us to cut corners but no one else.

The principles of a hand up and not a hand out, of honesty and personal responsibility and accountability, are widely held American principles. Yet you and I must, and do, acknowledge that there are some people who simply cannot care for themselves or carry their own weight. Whether by accident, accident of birth, or other unfortunate circumstances, there will *always* be some percentage of people who need care and that care is not cheap. It is hardly controversial that we need to, as a society, care for those who cannot care for themselves. Heck, even Republicons say *they* believe *that*! While I am skeptical of the sincerity of their saying it, when Republicons say that some people need to be cared for, they will do it in the cheapest and least dignified way—county poor houses, filthy public hospitals staffed by minimum wage workers in inadequate facilities. It is easy to be heartless when you push people away into dark corners and ignore them—out of sight, out of mind. What distinguishes *us* from them is that *we* believe in dignified, compassionate care, and "dignified" and "compassionate" are two words I *never* associate with Republicons! That this can be expensive is simply something we must reconcile ourselves to accept—some things in life really *are* more important than money. We have all seen or heard stories of poorly staffed orphanages or decrepit mental hospitals with scenes of people sitting in their own waste, rocking back and forth, or in fetal positions, drooling, with few attendants. I know that there are many places in the world where this kind of thing is happening. It is incumbent on all of us to try to stop it and make for a better way. We may not see that day ourselves, in our lifetimes, but if we can teach others and sensitize others to doing something about the terrible care of those least fortunate among us, then we can move toward solving these problems and, maybe one day, we can eradicate these conditions.

* * * * *

GROUP RESPONSIBILITY

For the vast majority of us, we are lucky. We are not consigned to poorly equipped custodial facilities, living by the grace of others. We can, and most certainly do, want to carry our own weight. We *want* to prosper. We all want the same things—a nice place to live, good food, proper clothing, the basic (or even nicer than basic) comforts of life. We want the best for our kids and to live as we would like, making choices that make our lives fulfilling. Sadly, there are many who view life as a "zero-sum game" meaning that when one "wins" others have to lose—there is only one pie and when one grabs a large chunk of it, all others are left with the remainder to divvy up. This is false. Take the example of plentiful, well-paved roads and a good rail system. Commerce is done better because commercial vehicles can get where they need to be; less vehicle maintenance is required because axles are not broken and front ends displaced by potholes and bumps; and materials can move on rail cars quickly and efficiently. People can get their kids to school and can get to work with a minimum of stress and expense. This is all for the public good. Of course, all this costs money and lots of it. There are those among us (we know who they are—don't we?) who say, "I don't want to pay taxes." They want all the benefits of a society, but not the burdens. People seem to have forgotten that when we build sewers and water delivery systems, they need to be maintained. When we turn on the tap and good, clean water comes out, that is not an accident. Someone had to spend enormous sums of money to ferry that water from one place to your tap. The water needs to be stored, piped and then disposed of after use. When toilets are flushed, all that stuff has to go *somewhere*.

I am the first to say government cannot be corrupt. When we pay for common goods—like roads, bridges and water/ sewer systems—the procurement, building and maintenance must be done efficiently and honestly. I am also the first to say that when someone is found with their hand in the public wallet, that person should go to *prison*. For a long stretch of time. A few well-publicized examples of that abuse, and a lot of corruption will end. It pains me greatly to see a lot of people in prison for drug offenses, but not for white collar crime. Take Wall Street. They brazenly stole hundreds of billions, even trillions of dollars, sank the global and U.S. economies, yet got *bailed out and no one went to prison; no one was even arrested or put on trial*. Simultaneously every day, people in poor neighborhoods (and we know what color skin they have, don't we?) go to prison for possessing small amounts of cocaine or heroin. This is insane. It costs us vast sums to lock up people (we lock up more than any other nation in the world), and we're locking up the wrong people. We seem to have a screwy idea that "business" is a legitimate way to steal (If I told you Wall Street is a crime scene, would that sound weird to you?) while more commonly understood crimes (like possession of rock cocaine by black people) are not questioned.

In court cases I worked on, when a lawyer coached a witness to lie and the lie was later exposed, or a lawyer withheld documents and the documents later came to light, there were no consequences. Judges just shrugged it off as if it were all part of the process. This sends a very bad signal to lawyers: They can cheat and profit from it. Just as companies that employ people who cheat Medicare out of billions of dollars need to have consequences visited upon them, both the companies and the individuals, so must lawyers who cheat and act disreputably. When war profiteers steal hundreds of billions of tax dollars in "the global war on terror" and nothing is ever done about it by way of recompense or punishment, cynicism and corruption are further spread throughout society and the very fabric of society corrodes. We all must be accountable for our actions, and sadly many of us are not. Even more sadly, many of us in positions of power are not accountable, and get away with it. This is as corrosive as battery acid. It breeds contempt for "the system" and encourages people to cheat, lie and steal since "everyone is doing it." There must be group acceptance of responsibilities we must shoulder as a group, and there must be individual and group accountability when things go wrong.

My motto is: "A hand up, not a hand out, and accountability for all." This means prison is for financial crimes as well as violent crimes; this means the "war on drugs" (or the war on people who use unapproved drugs) must end. Just as there is no "war on alcohol" or "war on tobacco" with prohibition and jail for offenders, there should be no war on marijuana and cocaine such as we have waged for decades. George W. Bush and Dick Cheney must be prosecuted for lying and torturing—indeed staging a grand fraud—to get us into Iraq. Their cohorts should likewise stand trial for their crimes against innocent Iraqis and the American people. War profiteering corporations must be held to account. Refunds are due and prison time is necessary. These efforts would go a long way to restore confidence in people that their government works for them, not just for the wealthy and well-connected. Likewise, when *government* fritters away money, it must *also* be held to account. Every tax dollar is precious and when government wastes money, it breeds contempt for government, drains away the legitimacy of government work, and gives ammunition to those whose agenda is to destroy government for their own devious ends. When stories come out about the Department of Housing and Urban Development wasting $400 million dollars on public housing, something *must* be done; people *must* be held accountable. http://www.washingtonpost.com/investigations/a-pattern-of-hud-projects-stalled-or-abandoned/2011/03/14/AFWelh3G_story.html?hpid=z1

It seems that most of us have long agreed there is a role for government, a real, substantial, legitimate role. A vocal minority wants to abolish government and give us anarchy but, of course, they only want anarchy in the *economic system*. Outside the economic system, these same loud mouths insist upon the government being big and oppressive, their personal property, their personal toy, to do with as they please. *They* get to decide what a woman can do with her body; *they* get to decide who can marry whom; *they* get to decide what people can smoke. These people chant "freedom and liberty" as mindless slogans without ever putting these statements into practice—except in the *economic realm*. These same people are totally blind to seeing that "freedom and liberty" means people are free and at liberty *to make choices* with that freedom and liberty, choices that are unacceptable to the same people who chant the slogan. Many of us view them as mere puppets of the corporate elite funding them because the corporate elite wants economic chaos while not caring about social issue dictatorship.

Government's legitimate role is seen in my life story: Social Security survivors' benefits, which benefitted me and my brothers when our dad died. The same Social Security survivors' benefits helped my dad pay for a roof over our heads after our mom died. A tuition-free public university education from City University of New York, paid for by taxpayers, allowed my brothers and me to get four-year college degrees and increase our earning capacity for life.

This, of course, means higher taxes paid to government, which provides a "rising tide to lift all boats." This does *not* mean that *only* government should be in the uplift business; private charity plays a very important role. I was given a tuition-free law school education by a private Jesuit (that's Catholic, for those scoring at home) university in Los Angeles, and that enabled me to become an attorney. The problem with private charity as the *exclusive means to uplift* is that it is uneven, random and often underfunded or conditional. By having a mix of government and private assistance—two ways to give a hand up and not a hand out—we as a society have a better chance of enabling the maximum number of us to achieve our highest and this way, we all benefit. After all, having someone work a good-paying job makes them a tax contributor; they have a much better chance of being law-abiding citizens; and they will help to perpetuate society rather than eat away at it. How many gainfully employed accountants have you seen mugging people on the streets? (That said, mugging people with computers and pens is a different issue and *that* is where holding people accountable, pardon the pun, comes in.)

Indelibly entwined with assistance (government, private or both) is the notion of individual responsibility and initiative. People simply *must* work hard to better themselves; get out of bed at a reasonably early hour; work at something to improve their lives, whether school or a job; and demand better of themselves than whatever their current circumstances are at any given moment. It is this balance—people taking responsibility for themselves and getting help—that maximizes the chances of a rewarding, fulfilled life, both economically and psychologically.

There is an old saying in the law: "My right to swing my fist ends at the tip of your nose." This recognizes that we each have "freedom," but the freedoms we have are limited by the rights of others. There has to be a balance. To put it another way: We are all in this thing called life together, and we can make it work or we can make it *not* work. Examples abound: When on the highway, you can choose to let someone who wants to merge ahead of you merge, or you can speed up and deny them access to the lane. "Road rage" can also be "road rudeness." When merging, use your turn signal to tell everyone else of your intentions. It is annoying, not to mention dangerous, to suddenly swerve into another lane of traffic. Likewise, while you have a right to a gun, please do not shoot irresponsibly. Of course, that deer may (and probably does) consider your shooting her irresponsible, too.

The days are long gone when we can live a Daniel Boone lifestyle. Going out alone in the woods with your rifle, and little else, to carve your living out of nature may be romantic in folktale lore, but it simply is not practical these days. Times have changed. You can certainly build camp fires in the forest, but setting the forest on fire is a very bad thing. Not only will critters great and small be killed, harmed or displaced but others, who also want to use the forest, will be damaged as well. There are little "woods" left, as we have paved over much of it, and there are far more people in the world today, putting tremendous pressure on nature.

We need "balance" and the courts often are called upon to do precisely that—balance the rights of the various claimants. For example, people want the right to publicly protest, the First Amendment guarantees it, but other people do not have the right to commit violent acts on those whose protests are met with disagreement. When Nazis marched in Skokie, Illinois, a largely Jewish suburb of Chicago, not only did they have the right to do it, but the Jewish residents had no right to pelt the marchers with rocks, garbage or any other violent act. Similarly, when gays march for *their* rights, no one opposed is allowed to commit violence upon them. There is another saying in the law: "The antidote to loathsome free speech is more free speech." The idea is for a "marketplace of ideas" to compete, with the better ideas winning out. In order for this marketplace to function, *everyone* must have the right to air their views, no matter how unpopular.

This is why the "Ground Zero mosque" in Lower Manhattan (which was neither at Ground Zero, nor a mosque) must be allowed to exist and even defended by those who disagree with its existence. This is what makes us Americans. While many claim it is in *poor taste* to place a Muslim house of worship close to the site of World Trade Center attacks on September 11, 2001, it can easily and equally be said that it is in poor taste to call homosexuals "faggots" and "queers" and stand near gay marches yelling epithets at them. It is likewise bad taste to have Nazis march in a Jewish neighborhood, or to circulate a picture of President Obama photo-shopped with a Hitler moustache and wearing a Nazi uniform. Ditto for George W.

Bush. Yet all of these things are legal. Simply because they are unpopular with one or more segments of the public does not give us the right to censor them.

✳ ✳ ✳ ✳ ✳

THE NEW POLITICS

These principles are the foundation of a new politics: A sense of balance; personal and group responsibility; a reasonable, fair tax burden, with government spending on proper purposes; and a group acknowledgement that we have common needs—roads, bridges, sewers, clean water and air, and uncontaminated food. An agreement, widely shared and understood, that the best social program is a job. A broad agreement to give everyone a hand up, and to care for those who *do* need a hand out. An agreed-upon condemnation of lying, thievery, waste, fraud and abuse accompanied by appropriate penalties. Punishment when one hurts another—physical and financial. A group agreement that reasonable regulations for the public good are valuable so that we can have our common needs served. A generally agreed upon goal to obtain energy from clean and renewable sources that work in parallel with nature, not destroying nature. A consensus that America must work for Americans and that good-paying jobs are needed for us here at home, and that investing in education is key to achieving that goal. A belief that government does not have all the answers and that private initiative is good and is to be rewarded, but that government has a legitimate role to play.

Often, those who claim their "freedom" and "liberty" are being stolen complain about taxes. U.S. Supreme Court Justice Oliver Wendell Holmes famously said, ""Taxes are the price we pay for civilization." *Someone* must pay for the highways; someone must pay for the police, fire and military protections we enjoy. We also demand parks; public sanitation; clean streets; clean water; pure food; and products that do not maim or kill us. We demand many things in our modern lives, things that we ourselves cannot provide alone. So we band together, contribute (hopefully, modest) sums of money to the collective good and have a concomitant right to expect reasonable services for our tax payments. Yet there are those among us who take the benefits of our taxes for granted, and still demand that they not pay for them. We see this recently with the rise of Tea Party activists who decry "government-run health care," yet they themselves enjoy Medicare, which is, of course, government-run health care.

If we are having a debate about the edges of these issues, about the scope or degree, i.e., just how far we want to go in obtaining government (group) benefits, then that is one thing. Yet so much of the debate now is cast (by the radical corporatists) in absolutes. They want *no* government involvement while they appear unwilling to answer the question: "Just how do we pay for your services?"

In Tennessee, a man neglected to pay a $75 annual fee for fire service. Due to this, Gene Cranick in rural Obion County, lost his house and all its contents and his pets burned to death. The house sits outside the city of South Fulton, and South Fulton offers fire service for the annual fee for people outside the city limits. They have been doing it this way for 20 years.

A better practice would be to add the fee to the property taxes countywide and let firefighters do their jobs rather than having to check a list to see if the property owner is "approved" when the call comes in. The neighbor next to Gene Cranick was on the list. When the fire spread, the firefighters kept the fire from spreading to the neighbor's home while "They put water out on the fence line out here. They never said nothing to me. Never acknowledged. They stood out here and watched it burn," according to Mr. Cranick. This shows how extreme the anti-tax people have become. Fire fighting is a group benefit and responsibility. It should not be allowed to be optional.

Prior to the Salk vaccine, polio (spread by a virus) caused devastation for many people. It was transmitted person-to-person; one infected person was a danger to the entire population of people coming into contact with the carrier. The same is true of many diseases, HIV, for instance. Tuberculosis is spread person-to-person by coughs and sneezes that send tiny drops of spit out into the air to be inhaled by others. HIV and tuberculosis remain huge public health issues today; polio has been largely eradicated.

The key words here are "public health" since one infected person can cause a tremendous amount of damage. It is impossible to wall oneself off from the air, the water and the rest of the natural environment. It is well-known that parents with young children are constantly battling illnesses their kids bring home from school. You may hate it, but the fact remains, we are all in one boat together. With the advent of modern travel, it is now truly possible (and rather easy) to have diseases spread globally in a short time.

Likewise, insects and their problems can be and are spread throughout the world with often devastating results. The Asian longhorn beetle has infested many parts of the United States.

Believed to be brought here in untreated wood products from China and other Asian countries, the beetle is ravaging trees throughout the United States and causing big damages to the U.S. timber industry. Also from the Far East, the Asian carp has invaded the Mississippi River and is threatening to wreak havoc on the Great Lakes. A voracious eater, this fish (actually two types of related fishes) eats up the plankton at the bottom of the food chain and starves the native fish of their food. The Asian carp were imported into the U.S. to clear algae from waterways in the South. They escaped, made their way into rivers and away they went north. One of the two types, if startled, will literally jump out of the water and can cause serious physical injury to boaters. A foreign invasion brought to us by globalization. Again, be angry, but reality remains— we are all in this together.

There is an attitude of "I have mine, to hell with you, you get yours" that allows these kinds of public health problems to spread. Born of greed and ignorance, people believe they can wall themselves off from the world. They believe they cannot get bedbugs (a new scourge from a former time), and they cannot be harmed by diseases. So long as all is well at this moment, the thinking goes, all will remain well. Of course, by the time damage occurs, the people impacted express outrage and demand immediate action. Now that it has hit *them*, it's a crisis. We can debate whether this is human nature or not, but one thing seems sure: People tolerate *a lot* of problems in other peoples' lives so long as they are *other peoples'* problems. Since Hitler analogies are all the rage these days, let's stick with the Fuhrer. Many people in Germany did not believe "it could happen here." As long as Hitler did not come for *them*, they averted their eyes and went about their business. This attitude is best captured by Martin Niemoller, a Protestant pastor who finally publicly came out against Hitler and spent seven years in concentration camps for doing so. Here is his quote:

First they came for the Socialists, and I did not speak out—because I was not a Socialist.

Then they came for the Trade Unionists, and I did not speak out—because I was not a Trade Unionist.

Then they came for the Jews, and I did not speak out—because I was not a Jew.

Then they came for me—and there was no one left to speak for me.

A 1935 book by Sinclair Lewis is titled *It Can't Happen Here*. In it, he shows how it can. Bury your head in the sand; be belligerent and bully your way into smug self-satisfaction. But facts remain facts and sooner or later, "they" will come for you—whether "they" are Asian carp, bedbugs, Asian longhorn beetles or Sarah Palin and Michele Bachmann.

When we add the basic policy prescriptions to the values and principles set out here, we have a winning platform for a new politics. We have the points that I believe can be the foundation of our new politics:

1. Tax fairness, also known as "tax the rich also"
2. End corporate welfare
3. Downsize the war empire
4. Stop outsourcing jobs, bring the jobs home
5. Clean up politics by getting private money out of it
6. Punish criminality in its most egregious forms like stealing from the public, stealing from consumers and committing acts of violence
7. Demand accountability from all
8. Have a clean environment

9. Have clean energy sources
10. Make quality education available to all
11. Have good jobs available to all
12. Have decent, safe and sanitary places to live for all
13. Have a car or reasonable transportation available to all
14. Have quality health care available and affordable to all
15. Have a decent pension for all

These principles can be the foundation for a new, broadly based and broadly agreed upon set of *principles and policies* that transcend both current political parties, and set us on the path to a new politics.

* * * * *

30
THE END OF LABELS
AS WE KNOW THEM

Maybe once, a long time ago, political labels worked as "cues" to identify people's views and beliefs. "Liberal" meant something; "conservative" meant something, and we can debate what those words meant back in the day. "Communist" and "capitalist" had meanings and still do today. Currently, however, many labels in popular use mean nothing, and worse, are bandied about as weapons meaning whatever it is people *think* they mean. This kind of sloppy argumentation gets us into trouble. *They* call *us* "liberals" and turn *that* into a dirty word. They *define* "liberal" to mean *anything* that is *not them*. Nice trick, huh? Just what *is* a "liberal"? We can argue that until the cows come home, and it is *totally* non-productive.

When alleged "liberals" want *small government* by way of limits on snooping by government through the Patriot Act, for example, and alleged "conservatives" want big government intrusions without Constitutional support, such as with Patriot Act snooping, then the labels have no meaning. "I believe in small government." The people chanting that slogan immediately want to take possession of women's bodies and decide who can marry whom. That is not small government. *The slogans are disconnected from the policies, and people believe the slogans without thinking about the policies.* We have to turn the use of labels into *specific* and *narrow policy statements*. That way we can invoke a bundle of emotions and views on issues that matter with "labels" that accurately describe rather than using these broad, silly, meaningless labels.

When we set labels aside, a large majority of us agree on many bedrock public policies, if we stick to *issues* and not *labels*. Having military bases all over the world—and the cost of them—is an issue, not a label. Americans don't like the cost of empire and don't see the benefit of having an empire, certainly at this immense cost. Big majorities of Americans believe in *tax fairness*, that everyone should pay in proportion to their income. That is an issue and also a label, but not "conservative" or "liberal." It is fact-based. The degree of taxation can be argued about, with debate about what extent of taxation is fair, but at least the debate and issue are clustered around facts and figures.

A large majority of Americans believe that taxpayers should not subsidize private, profitable corporations. "Corporate welfare" is an issue—a policy choice. Now, for labeling: Use the word "welfare," which Republicons have turned into an epithet, a buzzword, triggering emotions and beliefs, and images of lazy, criminal black people sitting on their asses defrauding government (i.e., the hardworking white taxpayer) and you can see how people are motivated by catch phrases, key words, buzzwords and slogans. No one likes criminals. Corporations are very unpopular now. Thus, as a policy, attack "corporate criminals" and maybe you have an effective label, *but* you *certainly* have a broadly popular policy! If we can move the debate to which payments are and are not "corporate welfare," we can engage people in understanding how their taxes are spent. We can move away from the vague slogans and toward actual facts and figures.

Huge majorities of Americans think via slogans. They take their cues almost exclusively from key words—buzz words. Whole bundles of emotions and thoughts and beliefs are triggered by a word or phrase. This is part of communication, but many Americans *substitute* slogans (and their *associated bundles of emotions and beliefs*) for actual political thought. Once *their* labels and slogans are clashed with *our* narrow policy statements—statements tied to *actual, real life, factual situations*—their slogans' vapid nature becomes obvious and *we win*. For the big government haters, take away their Medicare and Social Security and they suddenly *love* "big government." Let's take some other narrow, factual policy points and test them against "labels." What if a person is terminally ill with cancer, is in excruciating pain, has but days or weeks to live— every doctor confirms this—and that person wants the escape of death? Is it right for *big government* to force that person to live in agony until the eventual end? So called "progressives" with their alleged "big government" ways are actually the small government advocates here, and alleged "conservatives" being the big government adherents. People have "freedom and liberty" (great slogans) to drink alcohol and smoke cigarettes, but not smoke marijuana. Challenge the "small government" types with this and other examples and they descend into fact-specific arguments about why *their* policy choices are good, but yours are bad. This is exactly what I am advocating here, a policy and fact-based group of debates, but with broadly accepted and popular policy choices, like tax fairness and ending corporate welfare, as guides to the debate contours.

How *they* can defend legalized tobacco and alcohol (especially when their spiritual ancestors got alcohol banned via Constitutional amendment on Prohibition in the 1920s) is a problem they just gloss over or breeze past because it is a narrow policy issue that forces them into extremely uncomfortable analysis, with no slogans to help them out. In truth, there is nothing "conservative" about prohibition of marijuana. Is telling people with AIDS or ALS (Lou Gehrig's Disease) they cannot smoke marijuana, and are *criminals*, if they want to stimulate their appetite, an example of "small government"? Is stopping a couple in love from marrying an example of "limited government"? Let's fight it out on *issues* and strip them of their silly slogans.

We can, and do, live by slogans. Slogans can quickly evoke images and associated thoughts and beliefs. "Idle hands are the work of the devil." "Cleanliness is next to Godliness." "Haste makes waste." There are a million slogans that evoke bundles of thoughts, emotions and beliefs in us. Fighting "godless communists" or "socialists" are effective ways to communicate much in a simple expression and a quick moment. In a world where we are inundated with information, devices, and tremendous pressures on our time, we want—we need—quick communication and answers. In a way, we have become attention deficit disorder sufferers; we cannot quietly, calmly focus and stay focused on one thing, while excluding all else, for extended periods of time. This is called "thinking" and "analysis," and so many of us seem to do precious little of it anymore. I admire people who still read books. Of course, now they can read on electronic devices that make the definition of "books" change from the paper version (hardcover or soft cover) to the e-version. People who make the time to think, to delve beneath surface simplicities, to explore and challenge themselves and others, these are the people who are more likely to have consistent philosophies and beliefs, and are more immune to being manipulated by those who want their money or to manipulate them for power.

Comedian Bill Maher asks a provocative question, along the lines of "I know why 1% of America votes for the Republican Party; please explain the other 40%." The answer is manipulation through slogans plus keeping people uneducated and unthinking. Use of symbols (i.e., the American flag and the Bible) and slogans with heated buzzwords completes the deal. The top 1% of billionaires and global corporatists know that if they come clean and tell America the truth: "We just care about money and power. We will destroy you, sell you dangerous products, trash the environment and everything else in the pursuit of private profit. We will enslave foreign peoples, and you next, corrupt governments, exploit you, manipulate you, soak you and do everything else bad to you and everyone else for our own personal enrichment" it will likely *not* lead to electoral success for their puppet front men, the Republicon Party. In order to get majorities of people to vote for their front men (and make no mistake, the Republicon Party is a wholly owned subsidiary of Wall Street), they use social issues like abortion and prayer in public schools, manipulation of patriotism ("American Exceptionalism") and war to keep people focused on "enemies." They manage to do this whether it is the former "godless Communists" of the Soviet Union or the new threat, "terrorism." By effectively labeling those who they create as "the other," the abortionists, the gays, the gun control crowd, Wall Street can manipulate people to ally themselves with their economic oppressors.

Thomas Frank's excellent book *What's The Matter With Kansas* explains all this in great detail; I highly recommend the book to you. The effectiveness of Wall Street to bamboozle people who should not be aligned with the rich to align with the rich is an amazing example of mind control and manipulation. The use of slogans and manipulation of symbols go a long way to accomplishing that goal. Note that the slogan "Freedom and Liberty" is often conflated with *economic regulation of big business*, such that freedom and liberty *only* apply when government is trying to constrain the excesses of global, multinational conglomerates. The poor, the working and middle classes are told that "freedom and liberty" and *not* regulating corporations are *one and the same*, yet "freedom and liberty" do not extend to personal choices about intimate details of living life. Upon closer (or any) examination, the contradiction of this would be apparent. But the goal is to stop people from thinking and analyzing so the use of slogans and employment of propaganda to keep people in a prison of ignorance—in their own minds and with themselves as the jailor—is the job of the image makers, paid handsomely for their work by Wall Street.

* * * * *

31
TIME FOR A THIRD PARTY?

I believe the Occupy Wall Street movement has the potential to spawn a third political party. I also believe it can be a huge consumer power movement, getting millions of people to move in a coordinated effort to divest money from bad corporate actors, big banks (such as Bank Transfer Day) and support new, socially responsible companies like a new auto insurance company, a new health insurance company or a new credit card company. The truth, however, is that we should *not need* a third party—we *need* a second party, a *real* Democratic Party!

We should know we have a problem with the Democratic Party when Rahm Emanuel (current Mayor of Chicago and former Chief of Staff to President Obama) called us "retards" and said, "Where is the left going to go?". Taking us for granted is not a good way to treat your friends. Asking us for money, hours of work and energy and then abandoning the promises to us is not the way to a cohesive, healthy political party. Giving in to the other side and strong-arming your own side is a recipe for disillusionment and apathy. And that is the tale of the election of 2010. Disappointed, deflated Democrats punished the President and the Democratic Party by staying home. The answer to Mr. Emanuel's question "Where is the left going to go?" was "The couch." Instead of reading the true message of the election, the President went further over to the Republicon side and thus further splintered his base. Giving up the public option on health insurance; giving in to the Bush tax cut continuation; not raising taxes on the rich and corporations when he had the chance (2009-2010) nor during the phony "debt ceiling crisis" of July 2011; continuing the war; and attempting to cut Social Security and Medicare were but a few of the big disappointments of President Obama that have demoralized the base of the Democratic Party.

Likewise, many Republicans (I use the "a" here, for there are still some *actual*, non-insane Republicans) have given up on their party and either voted for President Obama in 2008 or simply registered as "independents" because they have given up on both parties. Many Americans perceive the two major parties as both controlled by the same corporate interests; a duopoly of essentially one political party with two wings— one hard core wing and one somewhat more moderate wing— but both agreed on the supremacy of corporate power and privilege. The time is ripe for a third party.

Third parties in America have a very bad track record. However, that does not mean we cannot try. Look on the bright side. With three parties, one party only needs 34% of the vote to win the race in our winner-take-all-system. Further, one can scare the living daylights out of both parties by getting even 20% of the vote. This kind of movement would put shockwaves up and down the spines of the two parties and could—key word "could"—drive them back to the issues that many Americans hold dear.

The key is to create an agenda that will draw evenly from Democrats, Republicans and independents. This way, a new third party would not split the Democratic Party and deliver the vote perpetually to the extreme Republicon Party. In order to siphon equally from the three groups (Democrats, Republicans and independents) a platform of broad economic agreement is essential. A truce or new consensus is required on the social issues. It is interesting to me that people are *always* focused on money. Many people play the lottery, people are obsessed with financial reports and people are always worrying about and puzzling over money, except when politics comes in and suddenly people care about other people's bodies, other people's religions and other people's flag burnings. The use of gay rights, women's reproductive rights and flag burning are *diversionary tactics* used by politicians who care about the money but want to divert people's attention away from the money issues, like where their tax dollars go. In order to avoid this trap, we need a simple economic agenda that appeals to the basic money issues like tax fairly, end corporate welfare, downsize the new Roman Empire we have built and create American jobs for Americans.

By focusing on these basic points, we can coalesce a large group of people around a simple platform that stays focused on basic money issues. We have a serious tax imbalance, we have a serious global war machine spending problem, and we have a serious jobs crisis. Sending jobs offshore to cheaper labor in foreign nations (and using "free trade agreements" to help promote this), while paying whopping amounts of tax dollars to gigantic corporations, is driving regular Americans crazy. People see the rich getting away with huge tax breaks, and this also drives them crazy. People see America literally crumbling under their feet while we are paying billions of dollars each week to support a global war machine that builds schools and roads elsewhere, and it drives them crazy. A new party that focuses on these and just these issues and has an agenda of setting these things right can have an impact and re-energize many demoralized voters. I believe it is worth a try. I definitely believe it is worth a national discussion.

As to Occupy Wall Street, I believe it can act as a pressure group to force the Democratic Party to be the real Democratic Party. And if it won't be, then OWS can find leaders from within its ranks to challenge the current dual system of two corporate parties, one less captive of Wall Street than the other, but only by a matter of a small degree.

I have gotten close to the Vermont Progressive Party, and believe they can be an effective model to force the now-corporate Democratic Party to be the real Democratic Party it is supposed to be. Unlike the Green Party, which runs a candidate in every election even when a good Democrat is on the ballot, the Vermont Progressive Party supports the Democrats when there is a good one, challenges the Democrats when there is a bad one (by putting a competitor on the ballot), and constantly talks to the Democrats saying, "Give us a real Democrat and we won't run someone against you." In this way, Vermont got a good Democratic governor, Peter Shumlin, who supported and got passed a single-payer health care system in Vermont. The Vermont Progressive Party also believes that its model can be used in other states, but not on a national level. I agree, at least for now. Let us start state-by-state and seed the ground with good, true Democrats. They will soon move up to the national stage. I would like to see the Occupy Wall Street movement spawn candidates to challenge the Democrats, and have those new candidates become effective political challengers to the Democrats while not splitting the Party and handing elections over to the Republicons who are, after all, insane, homicidal, sociopaths, totally captive to the corporate elite.

I would also like to see people like George Soros (who is so pilloried by the corporate side and their Republicon sycophants and front men) and people in a similar position step up and fund new companies that can be patronized by the OWS consumers. This would take business from the big auto insurance companies, the big health insurance companies, and the duopoly of VISA and MasterCard.

While demanding that government provide effective regulation of the marketplace, we should not lose sight of the power of new entrants into the marketplace along with the power of a mass consumer movement to provide the customers once the initial funding launches the new ventures. Simply put, the barriers to entry are very high and very expensive. To start a new insurance company, for example, someone or some group with access to substantial capital is needed to get the thing going. Once started, a mass consumer movement can provide the customer base. This way, actual competition can be created and, because the new companies would be limited profit enterprises, they would not be selling stock and not be beholden to Wall Street and "analyst expectations." The new companies can still be run efficiently, as businesses must be, but can price their products to return a modest or small profit, not giving incredibly high bonuses to their CEOs and other executives, thus undercutting the established bad corporate actors. The new companies can use the rules of a capitalist, competitive system against these older companies to siphon off their customer base and force them to actually compete. (Then again, the federal government could actually enforce the anti-trust laws that are already on the books.)

* * * * *

32
A MESSAGE OF HOPE

Let me wrap this up with a pep talk. It *is* necessary for us to hear it! For our side, we do not acknowledge just how much we have succeeded. For us, the glass is always three-quarters empty and the end is always near. For us, the sky is perpetually falling and the evildoers, the 'Cons, are always winning. Any advance by them has us throwing our hands in the air, gnashing our teeth and writhing in paroxysms of hysteria. Our sense of proportion and our sense of perspective are non-existent. What's worse, we don't fight back against the evildoers—we fight ourselves. We spend very little time recognizing our major accomplishments. We must demand our leaders defend the major advances we and our forbears achieved. Defend Social Security, Medicare, Medicaid, child labor laws, public education, environmental standards, civil rights laws and civil rights progress, plus all the social advances that have happened since the 1930s. *We have transformed America.* Women have rights that are still not equal but are a lot better than they were, and a lot better than they would be if the other side were in control. Blacks, gays and other "minorities" have advanced *far* beyond where they would have been had the other side been making the rules all these years. Just in the span of my lifetime (1959 to present), blacks and whites freely mingle at all public places, this was not true at the time of my birth, and blacks have many more visible positions of authority in society. We have food safety laws, work place safety standards, and a social safety net that we *forced into existence over tremendous opposition*. Of course, once created, these things need defending. The other side *never* gives up trying to repeal everything. We have to defend our gains and *simultaneously* push for new progress. Their goal is to repeal the 20th century; our goal is to move forward into the 21st. We are fighting on two fronts—get used to it.

Our side needs to refocus on reselling America on all the good we have done; a new generation needs to be educated and an older generation needs to be reminded. My life advancement was made possible in large part by Social Security survivors' benefits and free public college education. So many of us have attained a good station in life with the hand up not the hand out that America has provided since President Franklin Roosevelt moved us forward during the Depression. We need to be proud of the social advances we have forced, and we need to remind the other side that they fought each and every social advance that we all enjoy today. They opposed Social Security and called it communism; they (including Ronald Reagan) called Medicare socialism; they said blacks should not be sitting at the same lunch counters and stadiums as whites; and that women cannot be lawyers, doctors or business leaders. They routinely attack Mexicans under the guise of "illegal immigrants" and pander to the most extreme among them with racist statements about President Obama.

From the time of President Franklin Roosevelt until Ronald Reagan, our party was dominant in every way. America decisively rejected the Republicons and embraced labor unions and our entire agenda. The reason we have been back on our heels is because our *leaders* have not fought for our principles and priorities; they have allowed themselves to be bullied, and they have adopted so many of the 'Cons talking points and agenda. They have also sold out to the same monied interests that control the Republicon Party. We must demand better and be ready to replace the "leaders" who sell us out. We have much to defend and should remind ourselves of how much good we have done. Our rank-and-file has devolved into squabbling amongst itself and not unified around a central, smart, clear, crisp and strong agenda to take the fight forward. This can be fixed. One of the aims of this book is to do just that.

We do not loudly and relentlessly proclaim that the only reason a black man named Clarence Thomas can be on the Supreme Court is because of what *we* did. The same is true for the first woman on the Supreme Court, Sandra Day O'Connor. We do not go after Clarence Thomas the way *they* went after Abe Fortas (does anyone even know who Abe Fortas was?) for slamming the door in the faces of the very people who paved the way (and a hard slog it was) for their ascension. Clarence Thomas has committed so many ethical and legal violations on the Supreme Court that we should have our people in the media *every day* making a public spectacle of the man, but we don't. Our messaging is abysmal. Our focus is non-existent. This needs to change and *fast*.

Let me remind you of what our predecessors (and we) struggled through to get us all here. Slavery took many decades to abolish and took a terribly bloody Civil War to finally end. Abolitionists of the pre-Civil War period, for many decades, fought and despaired as to whether they would ever end the practice of one race of humans owning another while extracting the labor of their "property" and subjecting their slaves to an existence barely above animals. Think how the abolitionists felt in the years before the Civil War. They saw day after day, month after month, year after year pass with new states being admitted to the Union that allowed slavery. Abolition seemed like it would never occur. Did the abolitionists give up? No, they fought and advocated relentlessly.

Women did not get the right to vote until 1920. Women were advocating for that basic, simple right for many decades before it happened. Lucretia Mott, Susan B. Anthony and Elizabeth Cady Stanton (as well as all the other suffragettes) worked tirelessly for many decades to *simply get the right to vote*. Do you think they despaired from time to time? Of course they did, but did they give up? They did not. Think of how bleak the future looked for the abolitionists and the suffragettes as they struggled to turn the tide of public opinion in their favor. They could have given up. The work was hard and the rewards seemed far away or even non-existent, but they kept fighting. And they overcame.

Speaking of overcoming, what would have happened (or *not* happened) if Rosa Parks had simply gone to the back of the bus on December 1, 1955 in Montgomery, Alabama? What would have happened (or *not* happened) if she simply obeyed the orders to move to the back of that bus—orders issued by bus driver James Blake to make way for a white passenger—or if she had not taken the time to be a part of the Montgomery chapter of the N.A.A.C.P. (National Association for the Advancement of Colored People) and been willing to suffer the consequences of her action? She was arrested, lost her job and ultimately moved north. What would have happened (or *not* happened) if the N.A.A.C.P. was not founded on February 12, 1909 by W.E.B. Du Bois and others to fight for justice and equality? What would have happened (or *not* happened) if Dr. Martin Luther King, Jr. did not rise up and fight 90 years *after the Civil War ended*? It would have been easy for Rosa Parks and Martin Luther King to give in or give up; after all, the Civil War had ended slavery, but *de facto* slavery continued even into my lifetime. Sharecropping (tenant farming that left the farmers in a near-slave condition) and rampant official discrimination were everywhere in America until the Civil Rights Era began in the years after World War II. From Jackie Robinson breaking baseball's color barrier to the Freedom Riders of the 1960s, many individuals stood up to be counted, and refused to give in to time-honored ways of discrimination. The fighting paid off, but the fighting was required.

The history of union rights in America is the history of violent suppression of the voices of workers. Many workers fought, were injured and died trying to simply organize themselves into bargaining units. Colorado's coal mines were subject to union organizing, strikes and strikebreaking as early as the 1880s. The struggle lasted for decades and included the Ludlow Massacre of 1914. The Colorado National Guard attacked a tent city of 1,200 striking coal miners and their families. Women and children were among the many dead. "The Great Railroad Strike" began in West Virginia in the summer of 1877 and spread to Pittsburgh, Philadelphia, Baltimore, and into Illinois and Missouri over 45 days. Many died and were injured at the hands of federal troops and National Guard soldiers. You heard me right—*American workers were fired on, beaten and killed by their own government's troops.* Labor organizing and strikes in industrial cities of the north during the late 1800s and early decades of the 1900s resulted in violent repression, often by the police, and also often by corporate-hired thugs who were allowed by the police to commit mayhem. Many hundreds and thousands of people died and were injured during all these strikes. Watch the movie *Matewan* (pronounced Mayt-won, 1987, starring Chris Cooper) for a great example of what the coal miners went through in West Virginia in order to organize. People did not give up; they kept fighting. Mary Harris "Mother" Jones led *child labor strikers seeking a 55 hour work week in 1903*! Child labor was common and our now-accepted 40 hour work week was simply a pipe dream back in those days. What if those brave souls—by the many thousands—had not organized and fought and died for the good of those coming up after them?

And you want to quit *now*? Whether it was union rights, civil rights, women's rights (now LGBT rights), ending slavery, getting decent social safety net programs for people, our ancestors went through many long and bloody struggles to give us the world we have today. We take so many of these things for granted. And yet, when the Koch brothers and their cohorts score a victory here or there, so many on our side are ready to give up and concede the future to these evildoers.

And that is the battle—the battle for the future. Our ancestors knew they would not live to see the days of their greatest conquests, but their kids and grandkids would, and so we must take up the cause again, now, and carry the fight forward for the generations coming up after us. We are but small links in a long chain of progress. Demanding that all things we want must happen *now*, and without opposition from the other side, is neither productive nor realistic. I sometimes wish the leaders and rank and file folks from the old days could come back and see us now. They'd give us a pep talk that would *singe our hair*. You and I are lucky they are *not* here to give us an earful.

The good news is, the demographic trends are on our side. The number of "minorities" coming up behind us is making America look more like, well, America—a multi-ethnic, multi-cultural, multi-lingual group of people all united in the core beliefs of America—freedom and liberty. The old, white, Southern "conservatives" are literally a dying breed. However, they are training their heirs to think and act like them. Numbers alone will not win the battle for us. The youngsters of today are on our side, but we need to teach them *why they must remain on our side* and that it is *their* side too. It won't happen by magic. We must agitate, organize and fight—and the fight is ours for the winning—if we will just keep going!

* * * * *

CONCLUSION

After my long and very weird journey which continues to this day, I have drawn a few (dare I say profound?) conclusions. To me, the most fundamental conclusion is that the greatest trip any of us make is in our *minds*. For all the travels, physical and otherwise, and all the interactions we have, the big journey is the one we make in our heads. Our *feelings* are central to everything we do every day—the battles we wage, the progress or non-progress we make, all of the important things that happen to us happen inside our minds.

I have traveled over the same ground at many points in my life. Each time, the place looks the same, but how I relate to it is different. And that seems to be the key. Places are what they are, buildings come and go, streets either change or do not, but it is how *we experience the places* that matters. People growing up rich in one place will likely look back on it with better memories than someone who had a rough go of it or grew up poor. The places don't change, we do. The places exist as they are; it is how we *experience* and then *feel about these places that vary*.

It is probably no surprise that I spend a fair bit of time thinking of my parents, my older brother, and the aunts, uncles, friends and yes, pets, that have died since I was a child. We all do this to one degree or another. Looking back and measuring time allows perspective. We reflect on how times have changed and how *we* have changed.

After spending time thinking of my parents and my oldest brother, I fervently wish they have found their peace. I hope that one day I will find mine, and that you will find yours. I believe that together we can.

❋ ❋ ❋ ❋ ❋

ABOUT THE AUTHOR

 orman Goldman spent most of his career practicing law in the State of California. He developed a love of radio broadcasting at an early age, which was rekindled in 2006 while filling in for national radio talk show host Ed Schultz. Norm also provided legal analysis for Schultz' daily radio show and his TV show on MSNBC.

Based in Los Angeles, Norm founded Pro Radio Productions, L.L.C. He produces and distributes his own nationwide talk show and proprietary content to radio stations, on line portals, and smartphone applications.

Norman Maurice Goldman was born in New York City, the youngest of three boys. His parents both died before he was 12, which resulted in his spending his remaining adolescent years in New York orphanages. A strong work ethic coupled with natural smarts, a charismatic personality, and perseverance allowed Norm to graduate from high school by the age of 17.

Leaving the orphanage and striking out on his own, Norm took advantage of local, state, and federal resources to attend college while also working to make ends meet. The helping hands from various agencies allowed Norm to graduate from Hunter College of the City University of New York with a B.S. degree in political science after which he attended Loyola Law School of Los Angeles on a full tuition scholarship. By the age of 26, he had graduated at the top 10% of his class and passed the California Bar Exam on his first try. The help of government agencies shaped his opinion of government and the positive role it can play in the lives of everyday people, when administered correctly. "Government should provide a hand up, not a hand out!"

Politics and broadcasting have always been a passion of Norm's. He was involved in both, before and during his successful career in private law practice. At age 15 and while attending high school, he worked as an intern in a local New York government office and on a gubernatorial campaign. Still in high school, he was a radio engineer, news writer, and on-air personality for New York University owned WNYU-FM (89.1). He continued to work at the station throughout his college career. Also during college, Norm took an internship in Congressman Ted Weiss' office (D-NY), was hired part-time when the internship ended and upon graduation, accepted a full-time staff job with the Congressman. Norm worked for Congressman Weiss from 1979 to 1982. He also worked on many political campaigns—federal, state and local.

In 2004, Norm hosted his own weekend talk show on KLSX (97.1) in Los Angeles before being asked to provide legal opinions for national talk show host Ed Schultz. His ability to make complex legal issues easily understood and accessible made Norm a big hit with Ed's four million listeners. His warm, funny, smart and approachable style, coupled with an honest look at politics, and a logical, understandable approach to government led Ed to make him a full-time substitute for him when he was away. Encouraged by the response, Norm launched his own radio show in September 2009. He is now heard throughout the country on large and medium market radio stations including stations and web portals owned by Clear Channel, (IHeart Radio.com) and CBS. (Radio.com)

Noticeably different from the usual right wing fare offered by many, Norm's logical take, sound advice, and warm "human" opinion on topics affecting every American has been described as "unique yet honest," setting him apart from the legions of angry sound-a-likes offered by traditional national radio networks. His "rational" not "radical" opinions provide radio stations, their listeners and advertisers with a truly credible, highly entertaining alternative to anything offered before. Norm is "Johnny-On-The-Spot" when legal news breaks, which is often, because of his experience practicing law for 25 years. He's been in the trenches, handling the nuts and bolts of litigation for a variety of clients, and experiencing the legal system from the inside out. Norman, his wife Frances, their two rescued dogs and a rescued cat reside in Los Angeles.

· · ·

The NorMan GoldMan Show, where JUSTICE is served live at 3 p.m. Pacific, 6 p.m. Eastern daily. Hear the show LIVE ON AIR, ON LINE and download Norm's Smartphone App through Apple iTunes and Android Marketplace at www.normangoldman.com.

CPSIA information can be obtained at www.ICGtesting.com
Printed in the USA
LVOW010624090112

262978LV00002B/1/P